THE BUMPER BOOK OF USELESS INFORMATION

THE BUMPER BOOK OF USELESS INFORMATION

AN OFFICIAL USELESS INFORMATION SOCIETY PUBLICATION

BY NOEL BOTHAM

JOHN BLAKE

Published by John Blake Publishing Ltd,
3 Bramber Court, 2 Bramber Road,
London W14 9PB, England

www.blake.co.uk

First published in hardback in 2007

ISBN 978 1 84454 485 1

British Library Cataloguing-in-Publication Data:

A catalogue record for this book is available from the British Library.

Design by www.envydesign.co.uk

Printed and bound in Great Britain by Mackays of Chatham Ltd, Chatham, Kent

1 3 5 7 9 10 8 6 4 2

Papers used by John Blake Publishing are natural, recyclable products made from
wood grown in sustainable forests. The manufacturing processes conform to the
environmental regulations of the country of origin.

Every attempt has been made to contact the relevant copyright-holders, but some
were unobtainable. We would be grateful if the appropriate people could contact us.

As always, to my wife,
Lesley Lewis, with love.

CONTENTS

CONTENTS

FOREWORD

The idea for the Useless Information Society came some sixteen years ago during a memorable champagne lunch at the late, great, Soho restaurant, *L'Epicure*.

My guest, and good friend, the celebrated newspaper columnist, author and playwright, Keith Waterhouse, and I were swapping crazy suggestions about ways we could entertain our friends, when the idea of a club to promote useless information popped into my mind. Keith loved the idea and in minutes we came up with the name. He volunteered to be the Society's General Secretary, and we decided I would be the Chairman.

By the end of lunch we had devised a set of rules and drawn up a list of friends from the worlds of acting, publishing, journalism, music and art that would be our members. *L'Epicure* owner Nigel Tarr became our first. Celebrity priest, and close friend, Father Michael Seed agreed to be our Chaplain; and composer and pianist Kenny

Clayton, our Beadle. It was decided that he would wear a tricorn 'Mr Bumble' hat and carry a long wooden stave of office, to be used to hook the feet from under any member who dared offer an either useful or boring titbit of information.

Since then, the members, 22 in total, have met for Society dinners several times a year in various private dining rooms, after which each member stands, and in two minutes regales his friends with his latest titbits of useless information. My favourite, from a journalist member, remains: *'My grandmother's name was Gertrude.'* Simple, brief, and utterly useless. Perfect.

After the close of *L'Epicure,* the Society's spiritual home became the French House restaurant in Soho, though we have also enjoyed other locations, including the chef's kitchen in the Connaught Hotel, and one extraordinary feast in Archbishop's House, the palatial private residence of the head of the Catholic Church in the United Kingdom.

1

SHOW
BUSINESS AND
CELEBRITIES

—— SHOW BUSINESS AND CELEBRITIES ——

- Bing Crosby turned down the role of Columbo in the eponymous TV detective series before Peter Falk was offered the part.

- Michael Caine fell in love with a woman he saw in a Maxwell House coffee commercial. She was Shakira Baksh, whom he later married.

- Actress Joan Collins was 50 when she posed semi-nude for *Playboy* magazine. It was a sell-out edition.

- Dean Martin, born Dino Crocetti, boxed under the name Kid Crochet as a teenager.

- The film version of *Oliver Twist* had its name changed to *Lost Child in Foggy City* when it was shown in China.

- *Wayne's World* was filmed in two weeks.

- The Marx Brothers started their show-business career as the Six Mascots, featuring brothers Leonard, Adolph, Julius, Milton, their mother Minnie and their aunt Hannah. Later the brothers changed their names to Chico, Harpo, Groucho and Gummo (in respective order).

—— SHOW BUSINESS AND CELEBRITIES ——

- The first time Madonna appeared on the US *Late Show with David Letterman* her foul language had to be bleeped out twelve times. On her second appearance it only happened once.

- The term 'rock 'n' roll' was coined in 1951.

- Shirley Temple was only three when she appeared in her first film, crime drama *The Red-Haired Alibi*.

- The role that made Peter O'Toole a star, Lawrence of Arabia, had been turned down by Marlon Brando and Albert Finney.

- When Otto Preminger hired Kim Novak from Columbia Pictures for $100,000 to use her in his film *The Man with the Golden Arm*, she was still only paid $100 a week.

- Debbie Reynolds's daughter, Carrie Fisher, once said, 'I always wanted to do what my mother did. Get all dressed up – shoot people – fall in the mud. I never considered doing anything else.'

- The Bugs Bunny prototype first appeared in the cartoon *Porky's Hair Hunt* in 1938.

—— SHOW BUSINESS AND CELEBRITIES ——

- The late W C Fields once said that any man who hated children and dogs couldn't be all bad. He probably turned in his grave when in 1980 his home was sold to make way for a nursery school.

- The BBC once rejected a claim that Chuck Berry's 1972 hit record 'Ding-a-ling' (the tale of a young man who couldn't stop playing with the song-title object and invited his friends to join in) was intended to stimulate self and mutual masturbation. Quoting Chuck Berry, they said the record was plainly about a boy who was given a bell to play with.

- As part of his fee for appearing in *Terminator 2*, Arnold Schwarzenegger, was given a Gulf Stream GIII jet aircraft.

- The blood in the famous shower scene in Alfred Hitchcock's *Psycho* was in fact Hershey's chocolate syrup.

- In the early episodes of *Star Trek* Dr McCoy's medical scanner was just an ordinary salt shaker.

- Actor John Barrymore kept a pet vulture named Maloney, which would sit on his knee and hiss.

—— SHOW BUSINESS AND CELEBRITIES ——

- In pop royalty the Queen of Blues is Dinah Washington, the Queen of Soul is Aretha Franklin, the Queen of Disco is Donna Summer, the King of Swing is Benny Goodman, the King of the Cowboys is Roy Rogers and the King is Elvis Presley.

- Superman appears in every episode of the US TV series *Seinfeld*. There is a model figure of the superhero on a shelf in Jerry Seinfeld's apartment.

- The most expensive silent movie ever made was the 1926 epic *Ben Hur*, which cost $3.9 million.

- Peter Ustinov was signed for the part of Inspector Jacques Clousseau but pulled out at the last moment, opening the way for Peter Sellers to play the part.

- David Selznick, producer of *Gone With the Wind*, was fined $5,000 by the Motion Picture Association of America for letting the word 'damn' be used.

- The legs shown walking down the street in the opening of *Saturday Night Fever* were not John Travolta's but those of his stand-in, Jeff Zinn.

- Samuel Goldwyn's real name was Samuel Goldfish.

—— SHOW BUSINESS AND CELEBRITIES ——

- Burt Reynolds now lives in the Florida holiday home of Chicago gangster Al Capone.

- Don McLean's famous song was inspired by the name of the plane in which Buddy Holly died – American Pie.

- Sylvia Miles had the shortest performance ever nominated for an Oscar in the film *Midnight Cowboy*. Her entire role lasted only six minutes.

- Before he became a comedian Bob Hope was a boxer known as Packy East.

- The first custard pie ever thrown on screen was in the 1920s silent comedy *Keystone Kops*. Mabel Normand threw a pie at Ben Turpin.

- The first name of TV detective Lieutenant Columbo was Phillip.

- Doris Day turned down the role of Mrs Robinson in *The Graduate* in 1967 because she said she could not picture herself making love on a film set. Anne Bancroft was given the role and was hugely successful.

- Paul McCartney's mother was a midwife.

—— SHOW BUSINESS AND CELEBRITIES ——

- Al Capone was so pleased with the 1932 film *Scarface* he gave director Howard Hawkes a miniature machine gun as a thank-you present.

- Telly Savalas first shaved his head not for the role of Kojak but for the part of Pontius Pilate in *The Greatest Story Ever Told*.

- After turning down the role of Marshall Matt Dylan in the TV show *Gunsmoke,* John Wayne recommended his good friend, James Arness, for the part. It made him a top star.

- To open their first ever theatre in 1903 in New Castle, Pennsylvania, Warner Brothers Jack, Harry, Sam and Albert borrowed the 99 chairs they needed from the local undertaker. They had to be taken back for funerals.

- Tom Selleck, who played heart-throb Thomas Magnum in the TV series *Magnum, PI*, was not chosen by the girl when he appeared as a contestant on *The Dating Game*.

- Shirley Temple always had 56 curls in her hair.

—— SHOW BUSINESS AND CELEBRITIES ——

● Sam Goldwyn spent an extra $20,000 reshooting a scene in *Bulldog Drummond* because he didn't understand the word 'din'. He had the word 'noise' substituted.

● Spencer Tracy said he would only take the part of the Penguin in the *Batman* TV series if he was allowed to kill Batman.

● Johnny Mathis dubbed Miss Piggy's singing voice in *The Muppet Movie* (1979).

● In film-editing lingo R2 D2 – the robot in *Star Wars* – means Reel 2, Dialogue 2.

● The longest list of film credits on record before *The Matrix Reloaded* was for the 1988 film *Who Framed Roger Rabbit?*. There were 763 names. It might have been 764 but Kathleen Turner, who dubbed the voice of Jessica Rabbit, asked not to be included in the credits.

● Only one woman, Tracy Reed, appeared in Stanley Kubrick's *Dr Strangelove, or How I Learned to Stop Worrying and Love the Bomb.*

—— SHOW BUSINESS AND CELEBRITIES ——

● The part of outlaw Jesse James has been played by many great Hollywood stars, but the first actor ever to play the role on screen was James's own son, Jesse James Jr, in the 1921 silent movie *Under the Black Flag*.

● In all his film contracts James Stewart was granted the right to select all the hats he would wear on screen.

● Actor David Niven made his screen debut as a Mexican, wearing a blanket, in the very first *Hopalong Cassidy* movie.

● The only cast member of the movie *M*A*S*H* to appear as a regular in the television series was Gary Burghoff, who played Corporal Radar O'Reilly in both.

● In *Arsenic and Old Lace* staring Cary Grant, a tombstone shown in the film is inscribed with Grant's real name, Archibald Leach.

● Artists had to draw 6,469,952 spots for the 1961 Walt Disney cartoon film *One Hundred and One Dalmatians*.

● When Katherine Hepburn was a child she shaved her head, wore trousers and called herself Jimmy because she so wanted to be a boy.

—— SHOW BUSINESS AND CELEBRITIES ——

- Boris Karloff's real name was William Henry Pratt and he was educated at Dulwich College, England.

- Sean Connery has to have the tattoos on his arm covered by make-up when filming. The tattoos declare his love for his mum and dad, and for Scotland.

- MGM's first picture with sound, the 1928 *White Shadows in the South Seas* had only one word of dialogue: 'Hello'.

- Gary Cooper believed *Gone with the Wind* would be 'the biggest flop in Hollywood's history' and turned down the leading role as Rhett Butler.

- When President Ronald Reagan began using the term 'Star Wars' to describe his computer-controlled space defence system George Lucas launched a lawsuit against him to protect his film title.

- When in 1986 Joan Rivers appeared on national TV with Victoria Principal, with whom she had a long-standing feud, the comedienne deliberately gave out the actress's unpublished home telephone number.

—— SHOW BUSINESS AND CELEBRITIES ——

- More extras were used in the 1981 film *Gandhi* than in any other movie; 300,000 were used for only a ten-minute funeral sequence.

- Despite being offered $4 million each, Paul Newman, Robert Redford and Steve McQueen all turned down the role of Superman. It eventually went to Christopher Reeve who was paid $250,000.

- The first TV sitcom couple to share a double bed were the Munsters Lily and Herman during the 1964/5 season.

- After Harrison Ford's brief 1966 appearance as a bellboy in *Dead Heat on a Merry-go-round* he was told, 'Kid, you ain't got it.'

- Sean Connery once worked as a coffin polisher.

- The race around the Great Court at Trinity College, Cambridge, featured in the 1981 film *Chariots of Fire* was actually filmed at Eton College because the Trinity dons refused to acknowledge the movie in any way.

- *The Flintstones* lawyer who never lost a case was called Perry Masonry.

—— SHOW BUSINESS AND CELEBRITIES ——

- The original title of the television series *Charlie's Angels* was *The Alley Cats*.

- Film star Sean Connery represented Scotland in the 1952 Mr Universe contest.

- Roger Moore has it written into all his film contracts that he must be provided with an unlimited supply of hand-rolled Cuban cigars during filming.

- When Tom and Jerry made their debut in the 1940 cartoon *Puss Gets the Boot*, Tom was called Jasper and Jerry didn't have a name at all.

- Marilyn Monroe's last ever line in a film was 'How do you find your way back in the dark?' spoken to Clark Gable in *The Misfits*.

- Keith Moon of The Who inspired the Muppet drummer Animal.

- The full name of the Fonz, played by Henry Winkler in the TV series *Happy Days*, was Arthur Herbert Fonzarelli.

—— SHOW BUSINESS AND CELEBRITIES ——

- A real cruise liner, the *Isle de France*, was deliberately sunk to provide the dramatic climax to the film *The Last Voyage* in 1960.

- Oprah Winfrey's first name should have been the biblical name Orpah, from the Book of Ruth, except the midwife made a mistake in spelling it when she filled out the birth certificate.

- Boris Karloff's first film role was as a $5-a-day extra (a Mexican soldier) in a non-horror silent movie, *His Majesty the American* (1919).

- Ronald Reagan and his second wife, Nancy Davis, appeared opposite each other in the movie *Hellcats of the Navy.*

- Half the world's population has seen at least one James Bond movie.

- *The Muppet Show* was banned from television in Saudi Arabia because one of its stars was Miss Piggy. Pigs are forbidden to Muslims.

- According to Warner Brothers, Sam Peckinpah used more ammunition – 90,000 blank rounds – than the entire Mexican Revolution when he made *The Wild Bunch*.

—— SHOW BUSINESS AND CELEBRITIES ——

- In the original draft for *Star Trek* the name of the USS Enterprise was down as the USS Yorktowne.

- The real Butch Cassidy did not die in Bolivia but returned home, minus the Sundance Kid, and became an adding-machine manufacturer.

- Howard Taylor (brother of Elizabeth) was so determined not to take a screen test arranged by his pushy, stage-struck mother that he shaved his head the night before.

- All characters in *The Flintstones* had four fingers on each hand and three toes on each foot.

- Walt Disney had wooden teeth.

- Caesar and Cleo were the early stage names of Sonny and Cher Bono.

- Charles Bronson and James Coburn both turned down the part of the Man With No Name in the spaghetti western *A Fistful of Dollars* before Clint Eastwood was signed for the role.

—— SHOW BUSINESS AND CELEBRITIES ——

- Orson Welles was only 25 years old when he co-wrote, produced, directed and starred in the 1941 masterpiece *Citizen Kane.*

- The phrase 'cameo role' was invented by Mike Todd when he made *Around the World in Eighty Days* in 1955. He had a host of top Hollywood stars playing bit parts.

- Bob Dylan's real name is Robert Zimmerman.

- Debra Winger was the voice of ET.

- Indiana Jones's first name was Henry.

- Leonard Nimoy, who went on to play Mr Spock in *Star Trek*, first appeared in alien guise in the pilot of a TV science-fiction series, *The Zombie Vanguard*. He played a Martian in the zombie army.

- Spot, Mr Data's cat in *Star Trek: The Next Generation*, was played by six different cats.

- Rita Hayworth's real name was Margarita Cansino.

- Woody Allen's legal name is Heywood Allen, but his real name was originally Allen Stewart Konigsberg.

—— SHOW BUSINESS AND CELEBRITIES ——

- Arnold Schwarzenegger made his screen debut as Arnold Strong in the 1970 Italian TV film *Hercules in New York*.

- The roaring lion in the MGM logo was named Volney and lived in Memphis Zoo.

- Gene Autry was the only entertainer to have all five stars on Hollywood's Walk of Fame – that is, one for each of the five categories of film, TV, recording, radio and theatre.

- The Beatles song 'Martha My Dear' was written by Paul McCartney about his sheepdog.

- John Wayne began his film career in a series of western movies as Singin' Sam, the silver screen's first singing cowboy. Unfortunately he couldn't make records because his singing voice and guitar playing were both dubbed.

- The 19-ft-long Batmobile used in the TV series *Batman*, starring Adam West, covered only four miles to the gallon.

- Elton John's real name is Reginald Dwight. 'Elton' came from Elton Dean, a Bluesology sax player, and 'John' came from Long John Baldry, founder of Blues Inc.

—— SHOW BUSINESS AND CELEBRITIES ——

● Because D W Griffith wanted one of his stars in the 1916 silent film *Intolerance* to have eyelashes that brushed her cheeks, false eyelashes were invented.

● Three thousand rats were specially bred for the film *Indiana Jones and the Last Crusade*.

● Sylvester Stallone worked as a sweeper of the lion cages in New York's Central Park Zoo to pay his way while trying to break into acting.

● The first film to be released in CinemaScope in 1953 was *The Robe*.

● Popeye's girlfriend, Olive Oil, wore a size 14A shoe.

● The only X-rated film to win an Oscar for Best Picture was *Midnight Cowboy*. It was later reduced to an R rating.

● The initial 'T' in *Star Trek* Captain James T Kirk's name stands for Tiberius.

● Under the Motion Picture censorship code, which was effective from 1934 to 1968, a screen kiss could only last 30 seconds before being labelled 'indecent'.

—— SHOW BUSINESS AND CELEBRITIES ——

● The word 'pregnant' was banned by censors from the script of TV sitcom *I Love Lucy* in 1952 – even though Lucy was obviously expecting and her son's birth was a major feature in that season's episodes.

● Ian Anderson, not Jethro Tull, is the name of the rock singer responsible for such songs as 'Aqualung' and 'Thick as a Brick'. Jethro Tull is the name of the band. And the original Jethro Tull was an English horticulturist who invented the seed drill.

● Mia Farrow once gave her vital statistics as 20–20–20.

● The longest ever sword fight on film, lasting six and a half minutes, was between Stewart Granger and Mel Ferrer in the 1952 film *Scaramouche*.

● James Doohan, who plays Lieutenant Commander Montgomery Scott in *Star Trek*, is missing the entire middle finger of his right hand.

● Rudolph Nureyev once danced a *pas de deux* from *Swan Lake* with Miss Piggy on *The Muppet Show*.

—— SHOW BUSINESS AND CELEBRITIES ——

● *The Cotton Club* was involved in so many lawsuits before its release in 1984 that the director included the name of the winning lawyers on the closing credits.

● Arnold Schwarzenegger bought the first Hummer manufactured for civilian use in 1992. The vehicle weighed in at 6,300 lbs and was seven feet wide.

● Arnold Schwarzenegger paid $772,500 for President John F Kennedy's golf clubs at a 1996 auction.

● Jim Carrey's middle name is Eugene.

● Keanu Reeves's first name means 'cool breeze over the mountains' in the Hawaiian language.

● Steven Seagal is a 7th degree black belt in Aikido.

● Tom Hanks is related to Abraham Lincoln.

● Tommy Lee Jones and Vice-President Al Gore were freshmen roommates at Harvard.

● Robin Williams was voted in high school the least likely to succeed.

—— **SHOW BUSINESS AND CELEBRITIES** ——

- Actress Sarah Bernhardt played a 13-year-old Juliet when she was 70 years old.

- Although starring in many gangster films, James Cagney started his career as a chorus boy.

- Bill Cosby was the first black man to win a best actor Emmy.

- Bruce Lee was so fast that they actually had to slow down a film so you could see his moves.

- Bruce Willis's real first name is Walter.

- Charlie Chaplin started in show business at age five.

- Charlie Chaplin was so popular during the 1920s and 1930s he received over 73,000 letters in just two days during a visit to London.

- Cher's given name is Cherilyn La Pierre.

- Dan Aykroyd's conehead from Saturday Night Live was auctioned off at $2,200.

—— SHOW BUSINESS AND CELEBRITIES ——

● Harrison Ford's scar on his face was caused by a car accident.

● In 1953, Marilyn Monroe appeared as the first *Playboy* centrefold.

● James Dean died in a Porsche Spydor.

● James Farr (who player Klinger on *Mash*) was the only member of the cast who actually served as a solider in the Korean War.

● John Forsythe was the voice of the Angels' Charlie.

● John Wayne's real birth name was Marion Morrison.

● Judy Garland's real name was Frances Gumm.

● Katherine Hepburn is the only actress to win four Oscars for best actress.

● Keanu Reeves once managed a pasta shop in Toronto.

——SHOW BUSINESS AND CELEBRITIES——

- Mae West did not-utter her infamous line 'Is that a gun in your pocket or are you just happy to see me?' until her last film *Sextette*. It had been floating around for years and has always been attributed to her, but its exact origins are unknown.

- Peter Falk, who played Columbo, has a glass eye.

- Peter Mayhew, who played Chewbacca in the first three *Star Wars* movies, was a hospital porter in London before starring as the Wookie.

- Shirley Temple made $1 million by the age of 10.

- The first crime mentioned in the first episode of *Hill Street Blues* was armed robbery.

- The first actress to appear on a postage stamp was race Kelly.

- Tom Cruise at one time wanted to be a priest. His acting career got in the way.

- Al Capone's business card said he was a used furniture dealer.

—— SHOW BUSINESS AND CELEBRITIES ——

● Al Capone's famous scar (which earned him the nickname Scarface) was from an attack. The brother of a girl he had insulted attacked him with a knife, leaving him with three distinctive scars.

● Behram, an Indian thug, holds the record for most murders by a single individual. He strangled 931 people between 1790 and 1840 with a piece of yellow and white cloth called a *ruhmal*. The most by a woman is 610, by Countess Erzsebet Bathory of Hungary.

● Fidel Castro was once a star baseball player for the Univeristy of Havana in the 1940s.

● While at Havard University, Edward Kennedy was suspended for cheating in a Spanish exam.

● William Pitt was England's youngest Prime Minister at the age of only 24, elected in 1783.

● A short time before Lincoln's assassination he dreamed he was going to die, and he related his dream to the Senate.

● Abraham Lincoln died in the same bed that had been occupied by his assassin John Wilkes Booth.

——SHOW BUSINESS AND CELEBRITIES——

- Abraham Lincoln had a wart on his face.

- Abraham Lincoln's famous Gettysburg Address consisted of just 272 words.

- All US presidents have worn glasses; some of them just didn't like to be seen with them in public.

- Andrew Jackson was the only president to believe that the world is flat.

- Andrew Johnson was the only self-educated tailor. He is the only president to make his own clothes and those of his cabinet.

- Before winning the election in 1860, Abraham Lincoln lost eight elections for various offices.

- Former US President Ronald Reagan once wore a Nazi uniform while acting in a film during his Hollywood days.

- Former US President Ulysses S Grant had the boyhood nickname 'Useless'.

- Four men were executed for Abraham Lincoln's assassination.

—— SHOW BUSINESS AND CELEBRITIES ——

- George Washington grew marijuana in his garden.

- George Washington was deathly afraid of being buried alive. After he died, he wanted to be laid out for three days just to make sure he was dead.

- George Washington's false teeth were made of whale bone.

- Gerald Ford was once a male model.

- Herbert Hoover was the first US president to have a telephone in his office.

- James Buchanan is said to have had the neatest handwriting of all the presidents.

- James Buchanan was the only unmarried president of the US.

- Jimmy Carter is a speed reader (2000 wpm).

- Jimmy Carter was the first US president born in a hospital.

- Louis IV of France had a stomach the size of two regular stomachs.

—— SHOW BUSINESS AND CELEBRITIES ——

- Louis XIV bathed once a year.

- Louis XIV had 40 personal wigmakers and almost 1000 wigs.

- Louisa May Alcott, author of the classic *Little Women*, hated children. She only wrote the book because her publisher asked her to.

- Lyndon B Johnson was the first president of the United States to wear contact lenses.

- President Grover Cleveland was a draft dodger. He hired someone to enter the service in his place, for which he was ridiculed by his political opponent, James G. Blaine. It was soon discovered, however, that Blaine had done the same thing himself.

- President James Garfield could write Latin with one hand and Greek with the other – simultaneously!

- President John F Kennedy could read four newspapers in 20 minutes.

- President John Quincy Adams owned a pet alligator which he kept in the East Room of the White House.

—— SHOW BUSINESS AND CELEBRITIES ——

● President Taft got stuck in his bathtub on his Inauguration Day and had to be pried out by his attendants.

● President Teddy Roosevelt died from an infected tooth.

● President Theodore Roosevelt was the first to announce to the world that Maxwell House coffee is 'Good to the last drop'.

● Richard Nixon left instructions for 'California, Here I Come' to be the last piece of music played (slowly and softly) were he to die in office.

● Richard Nixon's favourite drink was a dry martini.

● Ronald Reagan was the only divorced president.

● Roosevelt was the most superstitious president – he travelled continually but never left on a Friday. He also would not sit at the same table that held 13 other people.

● The longest inaugural address by a US president was given by William Henry Harrison. It was one hour and 45 minutes long during an intense snowstorm. One month later he died of pneumonia.

—— SHOW BUSINESS AND CELEBRITIES ——

- The only three US presidents who ever had to deal with real or impending impeachment – Andrew Johnson, Richard Nixon and Bill Clinton – all have names that are euphemisms for penis – johnson, dick and willie.

- Theodore Roosevelt finished a speech he was delivering after being shot in the chest, before he accepted any medical help in 1812.

- Theodore Roosevelt's mother and first wife died on the same day in 1884.

- There has never been a president from the Air Force or Marine Corps, although Reagan was in the Army Air Corps.

- Thomas Jefferson anonymously submitted design plans for the White House. They were rejected.

- Thomas Jefferson, John Adams and James Monroe all died on 4 July. Jefferson and Adams died at practically the same minute of the same day.

- US President Millard Fillmore's mother feared he may have been mentally retarded.

—— SHOW BUSINESS AND CELEBRITIES ——

- When the First Lady Eleanor Roosevelt received an alarming number of threatening letters soon after her husband became President at the height of the Depression, the Secret Service insisted that she carry a pistol in her purse.

- All 17 children of Queen Anne died before she did.

- Anne Boleyn, Queen Elizabeth I's mother, had six fingers on one hand.

- Catherine the Great relaxed by being tickled.

- Elizabeth I suffered from anthophobia (a fear of roses).

- Elizabeth Taylor has appeared on the cover of *Life* magazine more than anyone else.

- George Washington had to borrow money to go to his own inauguration.

- King Tut's tomb contained *four* coffins. The third coffin was made from 2,500 pounds of gold. And in today's market is worth approximately $13,000,000.

—— SHOW BUSINESS AND CELEBRITIES ——

- Six of Queen Victoria's grandchildren were married to rulers of countries – England, Russia, Germany, Sweden, Norway and Romania.

- One of Queen Victoria's children gave her a bustle for Christmas that played 'God Save the Queen' when she sat down.

- Prince Harry and Prince William are uncircumcised.

- Queen Berengaria (1191 AD) of England never lived in or visited England.

- Queen Victoria eased the discomfort of her menstrual cramps by having her doctor supply her with marijuana.

- Queen Victoria's mother – tongue was German.

- The first thing Queen Victoria did after her coronation was to remove her bed from her mother's room.

- The Queen of England has two birthdays – one real and one official.

- The royal house of Saudi Arabia has close to 10,000 princes and princesses.

—— SHOW BUSINESS AND CELEBRITIES ——

- The shortest British monarch was Charles I, who was 4'9.

- While performing her duties as queen, Cleopatra sometimes wore a fake beard.

- Elvis Presley had a twin brother named Garon, who died at birth, which is why Elvis's middle name was spelled Aron, in honour of his brother.

- Elvis Presley failed his music class in school.

- Elvis Presley never gave an encore.

- Elvis Presley's favourite food was fried peanut butter and banana sandwiches.

- Elvis Presley was once appointed Special Agent of the Bureau of Narcotics and Dangerous Drugs.

- Elvis Presley weighed 230 pounds at the time of his death.

- Frank Sinatra was once quoted as saying that rock 'n' roll was only played by 'cretinous goons'.

- Jimi Hendrix, Janis Joplin and Jim Morrison were all 27 years old when they died.

—— SHOW BUSINESS AND CELEBRITIES ——

- Karen Carpenter's doorbell chimed the first six notes of 'We've Only Just Begun'.

- Michael Jackson is black.

- Paul McCartney and Ringo Starr were left handed.

- Sheryl Crow's two front teeth are fake. She knocked them out when she tripped on stage earlier in her career.

- The opera singer Enrico Caruso practised in the bath, while accompanied by a pianist in a nearby room.

- After the Popeye strip started in 1931, spinach consumption went up by 33 per cent in the US.

- Before Mickey Mouse, Felix the Cat was the most popular cartoon character.

- Bugs Bunny first said, 'What's up, doc?' in the 1940 cartoon 'A Wild Hare.'

- Charlie Brown's father was a barber.

- Cinderella's real name is Ella.

—— SHOW BUSINESS AND CELEBRITIES ——

- Daisy is the name of Dagwood Bumstead's dog.

- Beetle from the comic strip 'Beetle Bailey' and Lois from the comic strip 'Hi and Lois' are brother and sister.

- Goofy actually started life as 'Dippy Dawg', a combination of both Goofy and Pluto.

- Donald Duck comics were banned in Finland because he doesn't wear pants.

- Donald Duck's middle name is Fauntleroy.

- Donald Duck's sister is called Dumbella.

- Felix the Cat is the first cartoon character to ever have been made into a balloon for a parade.

- Goofy had a wife, Mrs Goofy and one son, Goofy Jr.

- Lucy and Linus (who were brother and sister) had another little brother named Rerun. (He sometimes played left-field on Charlie Brown's baseball team, when he could find it!).

- Marmaduke (the cartoon dog) is a great dane.

—— SHOW BUSINESS AND CELEBRITIES ——

- Mickey Mouse is known as 'Topolino' in Italy. He was the first non-human to win an Oscar.

- Mickey Mouse's ears are always turned to the front, no matter which direction his head is pointing.

- On *Scooby Doo*, Shaggy's real name is Norville.

- *Peanuts* is the world's most read comic strip.

- Pokemon stands for pocket monster.

- Popeye was five feet, six inches tall.

- Scooby Doo's first real name is Scoobert.

- *The Black Cauldron* is the only PG-rated Disney animated feature.

- The Flintstones live at 39 Stone Canyon Way, Bedrock.

- The most common set of initials for Superman's friends and enemies is LL.

- The movie playing at the drive-in at the beginning of *The Flintstones* was *The Monster*.

—— SHOW BUSINESS AND CELEBRITIES ——

● The name of Dennis the Menace's dog is Gnasher.

● *The Simpsons* is the longest running animated series on TV.

● Tweety used to be a baby bird without feathers until the censors made him have feathers because he looked naked.

● Walt Disney named Mickey Mouse after Mickey Rooney, whose mother he dated for some time.

● Walt Disney originally supplied the voice for his character Mickey Mouse.

● Wilma Flintstone's maiden name was Wilma Slaghoopal, and Betty Rubble's was Betty Jean Mcbricker.

● According to Pope Innocent III, it was not a crime to kill someone after a game of chess.

● Mario, of Super Mario Bros. fame, appeared in the 1981 arcade game Donkey Kong. His original name was Jumpman, but was changed to Mario to honour the Nintendo of America's landlord, Mario Segali.

—— SHOW BUSINESS AND CELEBRITIES ——

- Parker Brothers prints about 50 billion dollars' worth of Monopoly money in one year.

- Since its introduction in February 1935, more than 150 million Monopoly board games have been sold worldwide.

- Since the Lego Group began manufacturing blocks in 1949, more than 189 billion pieces in 2000 different shapes have been produced. This is enough for about 30 Lego pieces for every living person on earth.

- The longest Monopoly game in a bathtub was 99 hours long.

- The Ouija board is named after the French and German words for yes – *oui* and *ja*.

- The word checkmate in chess comes from the Persian phrase *Shah-Mat* which means 'the king is dead'.

- Trivial Pursuit was invented by Canadians Scott Abbott and Chris Haney. They didn't want to pay the £10.50 price for Scrabble, so they made up their own game.

- Values on the Monopoly gameboard are the same today as they were in 1935.

—— SHOW BUSINESS AND CELEBRITIES ——

- *101 Dalmatians* and *Peter Pan* are the only two Disney cartoon features with both parents that are present and don't die throughout the movie.

- A walla-walla scene is one where extras pretend to be talking in the back-ground – when they say walla-walla it looks like they are actually talking.

- All of the clocks in the movie *Pulp Fiction* are stuck on 4:20.

- Bruce was the nickname of the mechanical shark used in the *Jaws* movies.

- C3P0 is the first character to speak in *Star Wars*.

- Darth Vader is the only officer in the Imperial Forces who doesn't have a rank.

- Debra Winger was the voice of ET.

- During the chariot scene in *Ben Hur* a small red car can be seen in the distance.

- Felix Leiter is James Bond's CIA contact.

—— SHOW BUSINESS AND CELEBRITIES ——

- Four people played Darth Vader: David Prowse was his body, James Earl Jones did the voice, Sebastian Shaw was his face and a fourth person did the breathing.

- In Disney's *Fantasia*, the sorcerer's name is Yensid (Disney spelled backwards).

- In the *Return of the Jedi* special edition during the new Couruscant footage at the end of the film a stormtrooper can be seen being carried over the crowds.

- In the 1983 film *JAWS 3D* the shark blows up. Some of the shark guts were stuffed ET dolls being sold at the time.

- In the early days of silent films, there was blatant thievery. Unscrupulous film companies would steal the film, reshoot a scene or two and release it as a new production. To combat this, the Biograph company put the company's trade mark initials AB somewhere in every scene – on a door, a wall, or window.

- In the film '*Star Trek: First Contact*', when Picard shows Lilly she is orbiting earth, Australia and Papua New Guinea are clearly visible... but New Zealand is missing.

—— SHOW BUSINESS AND CELEBRITIES ——

- In the *Mario Brothers* movie, the Princess's first name is Daisy, but in Mario 64, the game, her first name is Peach. Before that, it's Princess Toadstool.

- James Bond is known as 'Mr Kiss-Kiss-Bang-Bang' in Italy.

- Jean-Claude Van Damme was the alien in the original *Predator* in almost all the jumping and climbing scenes.

- *King Kong* is the only movie to have its sequel (*Son of Kong*) released the same year (1933).

- *King Kong* was Adolf Hitler's favourite movie.

- Luke Skywalker's last name was changed at the last minute from Starkiller in order to make it less violent.

- More bullets were fired in *Starship Troopers* than in any other movie made.

- The 1st time the 'f-word' was spoken in a movie was by Marianne Faithfull in the 1968 film, *I'll Never Forget Whatshisname*. In Brian De Palma's 1984 movie, *Scarface*, the word is spoken 206 times – an average of once every 29 seconds.

——SHOW BUSINESS AND CELEBRITIES——

- The famous theme ostensibly from '*Dragnet*' was actually composed by Miklos Rozsa for the 1946 film noir classic *The Killers*.

- The first female monster to appear on the big screen was the Bride of Frankenstein.

- The first James Bond movie was '*Dr No*.'

- The first real motion picture theatre was called a Nickelodeon (admission was a nickel) and opened in McKeesport Pennsylvania near Pittsburg. The first motion picture shown there was *The Great Train Robbery*.

- The first word spoken by an ape in the movie *Planet of the Apes* was 'smile'.

- *The Lion King* is the top grossing Disney movie of all-time with domestic gross intake of $312 million.

- The longest film ever released was ✱✱✱✱ by Andy Warhol, which lasted 24 hours. It proved, not surprisingly (except perhaps to its creator), an utter failure. It was withdrawn and re-released in a 90-minute form as *The Loves of Ondine*.

—— SHOW BUSINESS AND CELEBRITIES ——

● The longest Hollywood kiss was from the 1941 film *You're in the Army Now*, it lasted three minutes and three seconds.

● The mask used by Michael Myers in the original *Halloween* was actually a Captain Kirk mask painted white.

● The movie *Cleopatra*, starring Elizabeth Taylor, was banned from Egypt in 1963 because she was a Jewish convert.

● The movie *Clue* has three different endings. Each ending was randomly chosen for different theatres. All three endings are present in the home video.

● The name for Oz in *The Wizard of Oz* was thought up when the creator, Frank Baum, looked at his filing cabinet and saw A–N and O–Z, hence Oz.

● The second unit films movie shots that do not require the presence of actors.

● The skyscraper in *Die Hard* is the Century Fox Tower.

● The sound of ET walking was made by someone squishing her hands in jelly.

—— SHOW BUSINESS AND CELEBRITIES ——

- The word 'mafia' was purposely omitted from the *Godfather* screenplay.

- When the movie *The Wizard of Oz* first came out, it got bad reviews. The critics said it was stupid and uncreative.

- A violin actually contains 70 separate pieces of wood.

- *Abbey Road* was the last album recorded by the Beatles.

- Andy Warhol created the Rolling Stones' emblem depicting the big tongue. It first appeared on the cover of the *Sticky Fingers* album.

- Beethoven's Fifth was the first symphony to include trombones.

- Don MacLean's song 'American Pie' was written about Buddy Holly, The Big Bopper and Richie Valens. All three were on the same plane that crashed.

- 'Happy Birthday To You' is the most often sung song in America.

—— SHOW BUSINESS AND CELEBRITIES ——

- In 1976, Rodrigo's 'Guitar Concierto de Aranjuez' was No 1 in the UK for only three hours because of a computer error.

- Approximately 60 circus performers have been shot from cannons. At last report, 31 of these have been killed.

- Because metal was scarce, the Oscars given out during World War II were made of wood.

- *Breath*, by Samuel Beckett, was first performed in April 1970. The play lasts thirty seconds, has no actors and no dialogue.

- Dirty Harry's badge number is 2211.

- *Dracula* is the most filmed story of all time *Dr Jekyll and Mr Hyde* is second and *Oliver Twist* is third.

- Every day more money is printed for Monopoly than the US Treasury.

- Godzilla has made the covers of *Time* and *Newsweek*.

- *Gone With the Wind* is the only Civil War epic ever filmed without a single battle scene.

—— SHOW BUSINESS AND CELEBRITIES ——

- In 1938, Joe Shuster and Jerry Siegel sold all rights to the comic-strip character Superman to their publishers for $130.

- It is bad luck to say 'Macbeth' in a theatre.

- Kermit the Frog is left-handed.

- Kermit the Frog was named after Kermit Scott, a childhood friend of Jim Henson's, who became a professor of philosophy at Purdue University.

- Miss Piggy's measurements are 27-20-36.

- The Simpsons live at 742 Evergreen Terrace, Springfield and The Munsters at 1313 Mockingbird Lane, Mockingbird Heights.

- The Academy Award statue is named after a librarian's uncle. One day Margaret Herrick, librarian for the Academy of Motion Picture Arts and Sciences, made the remark that the statue looked like her Uncle Oscar, and the name stuck.

- The literal translation for *kung-fu* is leisure time.

—— **SHOW BUSINESS AND CELEBRITIES** ——

● The most common name in nursery rhymes is Jack.

● The tango originated as a dance between two men (for partnering practice).

● Nick Mason is the only member of Pink Floyd to appear on all of the band's albums.

● The 80s song 'Rosanna' was written by Rosanna Arquette, the actress.

● The bagpipe was originally made from the whole skin of a dead sheep.

● The band Duran Duran got their name from an astronaut in the 1968 Jane Fonda movie *Barbarella*.

● The Beatles featured two left-handed members: Paul, whom everyone saw holding his Hoffner bass left-handed, and Ringo, whose left-handedness is at least partially to blame for his 'original' drumming style.

● The Beatles song 'A Day in the Life' ends with a note sustained for 40 seconds.

—— SHOW BUSINESS AND CELEBRITIES ——

- The Beatles song 'Dear Prudence' was written about Mia Farrow's sister Prudence, when she wouldn't come out and play with Mia and the Beatles at a religious retreat in India.

- The biggest selling Christmas single of all time is Bing Crosby's 'White Christmas'.

- The first CD pressed in the US was Bruce Springsteen's *Born in the USA*.

- The harmonica is the world's most popular instrument.

- The Mamas and Papas were once called the Mugwumps.

- There is a music band named 'A Life-Threatening Buttocks Condition'.

- The song with the longest title is 'I'm a Cranky Old Yank in a Clanky Old Tank on the Streets of Yokohama with my Honolulu Mama Doin' Those Beat-o, Beat-o Flat-On-My-Seat-o, Hirohito Blues' written by Hoagy Carmichael. He later claimed the song title ended with 'Yank' and the rest was a joke.

—— SHOW BUSINESS AND CELEBRITIES ——

- When John Lennon divorced Julian Lennon's mother Cynthia, Paul McCartney composed 'Hey Jude' to cheer Julian up.

- ABBA got their name by taking the first letter from each of their names (Agnetha, Bjorn, Benny, Anni-frid).

- Caruso and Roy Orbison were the only tenors this century capable of hitting 'e' over high 'c'.

- The song, 'I am the Walrus', by John Lennon was inspired by a police two-tone siren.

- As well as appearing in *Star Trek*, William Shatner, Leonard Nimoy, James Doohan and George Takei have all appeared at one time or another on *The Twilight Zone*.

- Captain Jean-Luc Picard's fish was named Livingston.

- Daytime dramas are called soap operas because they were originally used to advertise soap powder. In America in the early days of TV, advertisers would write stories around the use of their soap powder.

—— SHOW BUSINESS AND CELEBRITIES ——

● For many years, the globe on the *NBC Nightly News* spun in the wrong direction. On 2 January 1984, NBC finally set the world spinning back in the proper direction.

● If you pause *Saturday Night Fever* at the 'How Deep Is Your Love' rehearsal scene, you will see the camera crew reflected in the dance hall mirror.

● In the theme song from *The Flintstones*, the line after 'Let's ride with the family down the street' is 'through the courtesy of Fred's two feet!'.

● One of the many Tarzans, Karmuala Searlel, was mauled to death by a raging elephant on the set.

● TV sitcom characters rarely say goodbye when they hang up the phone.

● The characters Bert and Ernie on *Sesame Street* were named after Bert the cop and Ernie the taxi driver in Frank Capra's *Its A Wonderful Life*.

● 'Video Killed the Radio Star' was the very first video ever played on MTV.

2

ROYALTY

ROYALTY

- In her sixties, Queen Elizabeth I often sat in front of her whole court with her dress thrown open at the front to expose her breasts. No reason was ever given for this amazing royal display.

- In his personal prayer book King George III struck out the words 'our most religious and gracious king' and substituted 'a most miserable sinner'.

- Within minutes of delivering a speech on road safety, in 1957, Prince Philip crashed his car.

- According to the bible King Solomon had 700 wives.

- The Queen always writes with a fountain pen which belonged to her father, King George VI.

- It is a popular misconception that the royal family cannot vote in political elections. It is only the Queen, herself, who is not allowed to vote. Other members of the family merely chose not to.

- An aide announced Napoleon's death to King George IV in 1821 with the words: 'Your greatest enemy is dead, sir.' The king replied: 'By God, is she?' Believing his aid was referring to the queen.

ROYALTY

- Prince Philip keeps a collection of press cartoons of himself on the walls of his lavatory in Sandringham.

- Prince Charles used the pick-up line on girls, 'I like to give myself heirs' when he attended Cambridge University. Prince William's pick up line at St Andrew's University was 'I'm the next king. Wanna pull?'

- US President Richard Nixon tried to marry off the then, 23 year old, Prince Charles, to his daughter Tricia. Nixon and his wife even going to the extent of deliberately leaving the couple alone in rooms in the White House, so they could get 'better acquainted'.

- In official photographs for their wedding stamps Prince Charles stood on a soapbox to give the impression he was much taller than Diana. For their engagement pictures, on stairs, she was made to stand on a lower step.

- Queen Mary turned up at a 1938 Buckingham Palace party wearing five diamond necklaces at one and the same time.

- King George V described his ancestors, buried in St George's Chapel, Windsor, as 'a strange busload to be travelling through eternity together.'

ROYALTY

- After they had run a series of revealing palace stories Prince Philip described the *Daily Express* as 'a bloody awful newspaper. It is full of lies, scandal and imagination. It is a vicious newspaper.'

- Queen Victoria adopted the nickname Pussy, for her eldest daughter, the Princess Royal.

- In the 17th Century, King Charles II twice won the horse race, the Newmarket Cup, riding his own horse.

- All royal babies are baptised with water brought from the River Jordan.

- King Charles II's coronation was delayed because there was no regalia. Oliver Cromwell had sold it all and it had to be replaced.

- The heart of King Henry VIII's beheaded wife Anne Boleyn was buried separately from her body in a church in Suffolk.

- George VI, George V, Charles I and Henry VIII were all second sons who succeeded to the throne.

- Prince Philip wears contact lenses.

ROYALTY

- Clive Jenkins once said of Prince Philip: 'He's the best argument for republicanism since George III.'

- The British monarch with the largest number of illegitimate children was King Henry I with 21. King Charles II was a worthy runner up with 15.

- Nell Gwynne, always referred to her lover King Charles II as Charles the third. Her previous two lovers had also been called Charles.

- Queen Victoria often put on a Scottish accent when travelling north of the border.

- King George V banned his son, King Edward VIII, for a year from playing billiards, after he miscued and slit the cloth on the table.

- Princess Margaret was afraid of the dark.

- Prince Andrew refused to wear shorts under his kilt as a child to be like Prince Philip. 'Papa doesn't wear anything and neither shall I!' He would cry.

- Princess Diana was the first royal bride not to use the word 'obey' in her marriage vows.

ROYALTY

- Queen Victoria described votes for women as 'a mad, wicked folly.'

- Discussing public duty Princess Anne said, 'There is a limit to how interesting a forty acre field can be, in my opinion.'

- The Queen's description of Niagara Falls: 'It looks very damp.'

- The Queen Mother could play the bongo drums expertly.

- The sirloin was introduced when King James I knighted a joint of beef (a loin), which was particularly tasty.

- Queen Victoria was taught to sing by the composer Mendelssohn.

- King Edward VIII was an accomplished banjo player. He could also play the ukulele and once composed and played a tune on the bagpipes.

- Anne of Cleves was so different to the portraits of her he had been shown, that King Henry VIII asked courtiers: 'Have you brought me the Flanders mare?'

ROYALTY

- King James I joined his friend Philip Herbert and his bride in bed on their honeymoon night!

- Princess Augusta of Saxe-Gotha was physically sick during her wedding to Frederick, Prince of Wales in 1736.

- Queen Victoria told her eldest daughter, when she became pregnant, 'It really is too dreadful to have the first year of one's married life and happiness spoilt by discomfort and misery – I was furious at being in that position.'

- Henry VIII's longest marriage was to Catherine of Aragon, his first bride. It lasted 23 years and 11 months. His shortest was to Anne of Cleves. The marriage ended in divorce after 6 months.

- King George I of Greece used the huge ballroom of his Athens palace as a roller skating ring.

- The English Queen with the most Christian names was Mary, wife of King George V who had eight. Victoria Mary Augusta Louisa Olga Pauline Claudine Agnes.

──── ROYALTY ────

- The Queen Mother used to describe her clothes as 'my props'.

- When they made Prince Charles an honorary chieftain the Kainai tribe of Alberta, Canada, gave him the name of Prince Red Chow.

- Prince Andrew was nicknamed *the sniggerer* by his schoolmates at Gordonstoun. At the same school Prince Edward was nicknamed *Jaws* because of the metal braces on his teeth.

- At Timbertops school in Australia Prince Charles was nicknamed 'Pommy Bastard'.

- Prince Charles was named *Hooligan of the Year* in 1978 by the RSPCA after he had hunted boar in Liechtenstein.

- Queen Victoria refused to believe in the existence of lesbianism and scratched out all reference to sex between women in the anti homosexuality bill before she signed it. That is why female homosexuality was never prosecuted in Britain.

ROYALTY

- King Edward V reigned only three months in 1483 before being deposed. He was never crowned. His descendant, King Edward VIII was also never crowned. He abdicated before his coronation had been due to take place.

- The longest British reign was that of Queen Victoria who was on the throne 63 years and 7 months from 1837 to 1901.

- The shortest reign was that of Lady Jane Grey which lasted only nine days in 1553. She was only 16 when she was beheaded.

- Queen Victoria's funeral was the first royal funeral to be held during the day and the first to involve pageantry. Previous royal funerals had taken place at night and were strictly private affairs.

- In the past millennium there have been three occasions when three kings ruled in a single year – 1066 (Edward the Confessor, King Harold and King William the Conqueror), 1483 (Edward IV, Edward V and Richard III) and 1936 (George V, Edward VIII and George VI).

ROYALTY

- King William IV of England was also King William III of Scotland, William II of Ireland and King William I of Hanover.

- King Charles I favourite joke was to place his court dwarf, 18 inches tall Jeffrey Hudson, between two halves of a loaf and pretend to eat him.

- It is said that King James I became a lifelong heavy drinker because his wet nurse was an alcoholic and he received such copious quantities of the hard stuff through her milk.

- King Edward III died of gonorrhea, which he caught from his mistress when he was 65 years of age.

- Henry VIII and Edward VI also died of venereal disease. George IV and William IV both died of cirrhosis of the liver.

- After meeting the Duke of Kent jazz musician, Louis Armstrong, sent him a 21st birthday message in which he wrote 'To Black Jack, the sharpest little cat I know. Satch.'

- The Queen Mother's favourite television show was *Dad's Army*

ROYALTY

- Not a lover of the arts, King George II would frequently scream in his thickly accented English: 'No more bainting, blays or boetry.'

- King Richard II invented the handkerchief.

- Queen Elizabeth I banned all mirrors from the royal apartments during the last decade of her life.

- Princess Anne told an American press conference in 1975: 'Everything I've seen written thus far is a copy of every falsification I've ever seen written about me. Even the pictures are not of me.'

- Even when they dined alone, with no extra guests, King George V insisted on his sons wearing full evening dress – white tie, tails and decorations, including the garter star and sash.

- Six of Britain's kings were homosexuals. They were William II, Richard I, Edward II, Richard II, James I and William III.

ROYALTY

- Prince Philip once remarked, 'Constitutionally, I don't exist.'

- When Prince Philip gave away Hèléne Cordet, the television personality, at her wedding, and became godfather to both her children – it not surprisingly raised suggestions that they were his own.

- Prime Minister Gladstone said of King Edward VII: 'He knows everything except what is in books.'

- Prince Charles twice failed his Maths 'O' Level.

- William of Orange was 4 inches smaller than his wife, Queen Mary.

- Princess Anne once said she would like to have been a long distance lorry driver.

- The Queen named one of her horses 'Charlton' after brothers Bobby and Jackie who helped lead England to victory in the 1966 World Cup.

- In dire financial straits, when a teenager, the Queen Mother sent her father a telegram message reading 'S.O.S., L.S.D., R.S.V.P.'

ROYALTY

- Anne Boleyn had three breasts and an extra finger.

- King Edward VII had an American bowling alley installed at Sandringham.

- The last time the Queen curtsied was in 1952 – to her father's body in St George's Chapel, Windsor.

- As a prince, King Edward VI had a 'whipping boy' named Barnaby Fitzpatrick, who was beaten every time the prince misbehaved during lessons.

- Queen Elizabeth I had over 2000 dresses.

- The Bishop of London had one of his own, sound, teeth extracted to show Queen Elizabeth I how easily one of her own, rotten, teeth could be removed.

- Prince Philip quit smoking on the night before his wedding.

- *The Times* obituary on King George IV reported, 'There never was an individual less regretted by his fellow creatures than this deceased king.'

ROYALTY

- After the Duke died the Duchess of Windsor always kept a loaded pistol by her bedside.

- There is a secret station, on the London Underground system beneath Buckingham Palace, so that the family can escape to Heathrow Airport in an emergency.

- To prevent her secrets being revealed to snoopers the Queen always uses black blotting paper

- Queen Victoria was the first woman to use chloroform during childbirth.

- Richard II once had to pawn his crown because he was such a spendthrift.

- The Queen has a special car mascot – a silver model of St George and the Dragon – which is transferred to any royal car in which she is travelling.

- King George IV's nickname for his much unloved wife, Queen Caroline, was *The Fiend*.

- The Queen is an excellent mimic and sometimes entertains the family aping the Prime Ministers she has known in the last half century.

ROYALTY

- The last widowed queen of England to remarry was Queen Catherine Parr, who married Lord Seymoor in 1547 – her fourth husband.

- So anxious was he not to shiver with cold in case people thought him to be trembling with fear that King Charles I wore two shirts for his execution.

- Sometimes Prince Philip hides a radio in his top hat when he attends the Ascot races – because he hates racing and prefers to listen to the cricket.

- When Lord Harris first turned up at Ascot wearing his, now famous, trade mark tweed, King Edward VII greeted him with the words: 'Mornin' Harris going rattin'?'

- The Queen has ten residences available to her if necessary. Buckingham Palace, Windsor Castle, St James's Palace, Kensington Palace, Hampton Court palace, Balmoral, Sandringham, Holyrood House, the Tower of London and the Palace of Westminster – which is still one of the monarch's official residences.

3

HISTORY

--- **HISTORY** ---

- A 200-year-old piece of Tibetan cheese was auctioned off for $1,513 in 1993.

- A B-25 bomber airplane crashed into the 79th floor of the Empire State Building on 28 July, 1945.

- A golden razor removed from King Tut's tomb was still sharp enough to be used.

- Abdul Kassam Ismael, Grand Vizier of Persia in the tenth century, carried his library with him wherever he went. The 117,000 volumes were carried by 400 camels trained to walk in alphabetical order.

- Acting was once considered evil, and actors in the first English play to be performed in America were arrested.

- Ancient Sybarites taught their horses to dance to music to make their parades more glamorous.

- Any Russian man who wore a beard was required to pay a special tax during the time of Peter the Great.

- At the turn of the last millennium, Dublin had the largest slave market in the world, run by the Vikings.

--- **HISTORY** ---

- Aztec emperor Montezuma had a nephew, Cuitlahac, whose name meant 'plenty of excrement'.

- Before the 1800's there were no separately designed shoes for right and left feet.

- Children in the Chinook Indian tribe were strapped between boards from head to toe so that they would have fashionably flat skulls.

- Czar Paul I banished soldiers to Siberia for marching out of step.

- Dinner guests during the medieval times in England were expected to bring their own knives to the table.

- In 18th – century France, visitors to the royal palace in Versailles were allowed to stand in a roped-off section of the main dining room and watch the king and queen eat.

- During the Cambrian period, about 500 million years ago, a day was only 20.6 hours long.

- During the eighteenth century, books that were considered offensive were sometimes punished by being whipped.

HISTORY

- During the Middle Ages, few people were able to read or write. The clergy were virtually the only ones that could.

- Everyone believed in the Middle Ages – as Aristotle had – that the heart was the seat of intelligence.

- Evidence of shoemaking exists as early as 10,000 BC.

- If a family had two servants or less in the US. in 1900, census takers recorded it as lower middle-class.

- If we had the same mortality rate as in the 1900s, more than half the people in the world today would not be alive.

- In 1281, the Mongol army of Kublai Khan tried to invade Japan but were ravaged by a hurricane that destroyed their fleet.

- In 1778, fashionable women of Paris never went out in blustery weather without a lightning rod attached to their hats.

- In 1801, 20 per cent of the people in the US were slaves.

- In 1900, the third leading cause of death was diarrhoea.

HISTORY

- In 1917, Margaret Sanger was jailed for one month for establishing the first birth control clinic.

- In ancient Egypt, killing a cat was a crime punishable by death.

- In certain parts of India and ancient China mouse meat was considered a delicacy.

- In medieval England, beer was often served with breakfast.

- In the 1700s in London you could purchase insurance against going to hell.

- In the 19th century, the British Navy attempted to dispel the superstition that Friday was an unlucky day to embark on a ship. The keel of a new ship was laid on a Friday; she was named HMS *Friday*, commanded by a Captain Friday and finally went to sea on a Friday. Neither the ship nor her crew were ever heard of again.

- In the marriage ceremony of the ancient Inca Indians of Peru, the couple was considered officially wed when they took off their sandals and handed them to each other.

HISTORY

● In Turkey, in the 16th and 17th centuries, anyone caught drinking coffee was put to death.

● In Victorian times, there was an intense fear of being buried alive, so when someone died, a small hole was dug from the casket to the surface, then a string was tied around the dead person's finger which was then attached to a small but loud bell that was hung on the surface of the grave, so that if someone was buried alive, they could ring the bell and whoever was on duty would go and dig them up. Someone was on the duty 24 hours a day – hence the graveyard shift.

● Income tax was first introduced in England in 1799 by British Prime Minister William Pitt.

● It costs more to buy a car today than it cost Christopher Columbus to equip and undertake three voyages to the New World.

● It has been calculated that in the last 3,500 years there have been only 230 years of peace throughout the civilized world.

● Leif Erikson was the first European to set foot in North America in the year 1000, NOT Columbus.

HISTORY

- It is estimated that within 20 years of Columbus discovering the New World the Spaniards killed off 1.5 million Indians.

- Native Americans never actually ate turkey; killing such a timid bird was thought to indicate laziness.

- New Zealand was the first country to give woman the vote in 1890.

- Olive oil was used for washing the body in the ancient Mediterranean world.

- Over 150 people were tried as witches and wizards in Salam, Massachusetts in the late 1600s.

- Pilgrims ate popcorn at the first Thanksgiving dinner.

- Pirates thought having an earring would improve their eyesight.

- Pope Paul IV, who was elected on 23 May 1555, was so outraged when he saw the naked bodies on the ceiling of the Sistene Chapel that he ordered Michelangelo to paint on to them.

HISTORY

- Sumerians (from 5000 BC) thought that the liver made blood and the heart was the centre of thought.

- The ancient Etruscans painted women white and men red in the wall paintings they used to decorate tombs.

- *The Bird of Prey* was the name of the Wright brothers' first plane.

- The Civil War was the first war in which news from the front was published within hours of its occurrence.

- The earliest recorded case of a man giving up smoking was on 5 April, 1679, when Johan Katsu, Sheriff of Turku, Finland, wrote in his diary, 'I quit smoking tobacco.' He died one month later.

- The first American in space was Alan B. Shepard Jr.

- The origin of the most used four-letter word: in Irish police stations in the 19th century – when public indecency was a serious crime – couples were charged with being Found Under Carnal Knowledge. Police abbreviated it to its initials and called it a F U C K. charge.

HISTORY

- The first police force was established in Paris in the year 1667.

- The guards of some of the emperors of Byzantium were Vikings.

- The Hundred Years War lasted for 116 years.

- The Japanese anthem has the oldest lyrics/text from the ninth century, but the music is from 1880.

- The name of Charles Darwin's survey ship was *The Beagle*.

- The name of the asteroid that was believed to have killed the dinosaurs was named Chixalub (pronounced Sheesh-uh-loob).

- The Nobel Prize resulted from a late change in the will of Alfred Nobel, who did not want to be remembered after his death as a propagator of violence – he invented dynamite.

- The Nobel Prize was first awarded in 1901.

- The ruins of Troy are located in Turkey.

HISTORY

- The shortest war in history was between Zanzibar and England in 1896. Zanzibar surrendered after 38 minutes.

- The Spanish Inquisition once condemned the entire Netherlands to death for heresy.

- The Toltecs, seventh-century native Mexicans, went to battle with wooden swords so as not to kill their enemies.

- There was a pony express in Persia many centuries before Christ. Riders on this ancient circuit, wearing special coloured headbands, delivered the mail across the vast stretch of Asia Minor, sometimes riding for hundreds of miles without a break.

- There were no ponies in the Pony Express.

- Those condemned to die by the axe in medieval and Renaissance England were obliged to tip their executioner to ensure that he would complete the job in one blow. In some executions, notably that of Mary, Queen of Scots, it took 15 whacks of the blade before the head was severed.

- To strengthen the Damascus sword, the blade was plunged into a slave.

HISTORY

- Until the Middle Ages, underwater divers near the Mediterranean coastline collected golden strands from the pen shell, which used the strands to hold itself in place. The strands were woven into a luxury textile and made into ladies' gloves so fine that a pair could be packed into an empty walnut shell.

- Vikings used the skulls of their enemies as drinking vessels.

- When Saigon fell the signal for all Americans to evacuate was Bing Crosby's 'White Christmas' being played on the radio.

- When the *Titanic* sunk there was 7,500lbs of ham on it.

- Slaves under the last emperors of China wore pigtails so they could be picked out quickly.

- The Chinese ideogram for 'trouble' depicts two women living under one roof.

- The Great Wall of China, which is over 2,500 miles, took over 1,700 years to build.

- There is enough stone in the Great Wall of China to build an eight-foot wall encircling the globe at the equator.

HISTORY

- The sinking of the German vessel *Wilhelm Gustloff* is the greatest sea disaster of all time. Close to 8,000 people drowned.

- About 300 years ago, most Egyptians died by the time they were 30.

- According to the Greek historian Herodotus, Egyptian men never became bald. The reason for this, Herodotus claimed, was that as children Egyptian males had their heads shaved, and their scalps were continually exposed to the health-giving rays of the sun.

- Ancient Egyptians shaved off their eyebrows to mourn the death of their cats.

- Ancient Egyptians slept on pillows made of stone.

- Cleopatra married two of her brothers.

- Dead Egyptian noblewomen were given the special treatment of being allowed a few days to ripen, so that the embalmers wouldn't find them too attractive.

- If a surgeon in ancient Egypt lost a patient while performing an operation, his hands were cut off.

HISTORY

- Egyptians once worshipped cats.

- In ancient Egypt, the apricot was called the egg of the sun.

- In Egypt, around 1500 BC. a shaved head was considered the ultimate in feminine beauty. Egyptian women removed every hair from their heads with special gold tweezers and polished their scalps to a high sheen with buffing cloths.

- On some mummies that have been unwrapped, the total length of the bandages has been about 1.5 miles.

- Preparing an Egyptian mummy sometimes took up to 70 days.

- Ra was the sun god of ancient Egypt.

- Ramses II, a pharaoh of Egypt died in 1225 BC. At the time of his death, he had fathered 111 sons and 67 daughters.

- The Egyptian hieroglyph for 100,000 is a tadpole.

- The first known contraceptive was crocodile dung, used by Egyptians in 2000 B.C.

HISTORY

- In English gambling dens, they used to have employees whose job was to swallow the dice if the police arrived.

- Aristarchus was the first greek astronomer in 290 BC. to suggest that the sun was the centre of the solar system.

- At the height of its power, in 400 BC, the Greek city of Sparta had 25,000 citizens and 500,000 slaves.

- In ancient Greece, women counted their age from the date they were married.

- Trivia is the Roman goddess of sorcery, hounds and the crossroads.

- In ancient Japan public contests were held to see who in a town could break wind loudest and longest. Winners were awarded many prizes and received great acclaim.

- After the great fire of Rome in 64 AD, the emperor Nero ostensibly decided to lay the blame on Christians residing in the city of Rome. These he gathered together, crucified, covered in pitch (tar) and burned alive. He walked around his gardens admiring the view.

HISTORY

- Flamingo tongues were a common delicacy at Roman feasts.

- In ancient Rome, weasels were used to catch mice.

- Julius Caesar tried to beef up the population of Rome by offering rewards to couples who had many children.

- The Pantheon is the largest building from ancient Rome that survives intact.

- The Roman emperor Caligula made his horse a senator.

- The Roman emperor Commodos collected all the dwarfs, cripples and freaks he could find in the city of Rome and had them brought to the Colosseum, where they were ordered to fight each other to the death with meat cleavers.

- The term 'It's all fun and games until someone loses an eye', is from ancient Rome. The only rule during wrestling matches was no eye gouging. Everything else was allowed but the only way to be disqualified was to poke someone's eyes out.

- Two dogs were among the *Titanic* survivors.

HISTORY

- During the First World War cigarettes were handed out to soldiers along with their rations.

- During World War I, 13,700,000 people died in battle.

- The first aerial photograph was taken from a balloon during the US Civil War.

- During conscription for World War II, there were nine documented cases of men with three testicles.

- During World War II, it took the US only four days to build a ship.

- During World War II, the Navajo language was used successfully as a code by the US.

- During World War II, Americans tried to train bats to drop bombs.

- Escape maps, compasses and files were inserted into Monopoly game boards and smuggled into POW camps inside Germany during World War II; real money for escapees was slipped into the packs of Monopoly money.

HISTORY

- Playing cards were issued to British pilots in World War II. If captured, they could be soaked in water and unfolded to reveal a map for escape.

- Prior to World War II, when guards were posted at the fence, anyone could wander right up to the front door of the US President's residence the White House.

- The term 'the whole nine yards' came from World War II fighter pilots in the Pacific. When arming their planes on the ground, the .50-calibre machine gun ammo belts measured exactly 27 feet before being loaded into the fuselage. If the pilots fired all their ammo at a target, it got the whole nine yards.

- The very first bomb dropped by the Allies on Berlin during World War II killed the only elephant in the Berlin Zoo.

- World War II involved over 57 countries.

4

SCIENCE AND NATURE

SCIENCE AND NATURE

- A bird has to fly at a minimum speed of 11 mph (18 kph) to be able to keep itself aloft.

- Americans use 16,000 tons (16,256 tonnes) of aspirin each year.

- Dogs can suffer from tonsillitis but not appendicitis as they don't have an appendix.

- Banging your head against a wall uses 150 calories an hour.

- The dumbest dogs in the world are Afghan hounds.

- The May fly lives only six hours, but its eggs take three years to hatch.

- Intelligent people have more zinc and copper in their hair.

- The sloth can starve to death even with a plentiful supply of food if there are too many cloudy days in a row. It needs sunshine to raise its body temperature so that the bacteria in its stomach are warm enough to digest the food it eats. It can take up to four days to digest even a single stomachful of food.

SCIENCE AND NATURE

- The housefly hums in the middle octave of the key of F.

- Crocodiles cannot stick their tongues out.

- A snail can sleep for three years.

- There are at least 100,000 chemical reactions going on in a normal human brain every second.

- City dogs live about three years longer than country dogs.

- A Laforte fracture is a fracture of all facial bones.

- During pregnancy a woman's blood volume can increase by up to 50% to a total of twelve pints. This is in reserve against possible loss of blood during delivery.

- Vets at London Zoo once fitted a snake with a glass eye.

- The brachiosaurus had a heart the size of a pick-up truck.

- Drinking water after eating reduces the acid in your mouth by 61%.

SCIENCE AND NATURE

- Other than humans black lemurs are the only primates that may have blue eyes.

- The average human bladder can hold 13 fluid ounces (approx. 0.4 litres) of liquid.

- Bacteria increase from one to one billion in a Petri dish in 24 hours.

- Rabbits can run at up to 45 mph (72 kph).

- Liquid helium, at a temperature just above absolute zero, can flow upwards.

- Although there are an estimated ten trillion stars in our galaxy, only some 3,000 of them are visible with the naked eye from earth.

- Glass is a highly viscous liquid.

- The miacis, the ancestor of the dog, had retractable claws and climbed trees when it roamed the earth 40 million years ago.

- Only one satellite has ever been destroyed by a meteor – the European Space Agency's *Olympus* in 1993.

————— **SCIENCE AND NATURE** —————

- The largest order of mammals is rodents with about 1,700 species.

- Any free-moving liquid will form itself into a sphere in outer space because of its surface tension.

- The black-and-white spots of Holstein dairy cattle are like fingerprints: no two cows have the same pattern of spots.

- The California sea otter grasps its mate's nose in its teeth while copulating.

- The sperm whale's brain weighs up to 20 lb (9 kg), which is six times heavier than a human's and is the heaviest of all the mammals.

- We still retain some of our caveman ancestors' reactions. That is why our hair stands on end when we are frightened: it is a reaction meant to scare off your enemy by making you look taller.

- Following one appeal in Kent for people to hand in all their unused drugs, enough strychnine was handed in on one day in Folkestone to kill the entire population of East Kent.

SCIENCE AND NATURE

- Jumping spiders have been found at a height of 22,000 ft (6,705 m) on Mount Everest.

- The majority of spiders belong to the 'orb weaver' spider family Aranidae – pronounced 'a rainy day'.

- A starfish doesn't have a brain.

- A lion's roar can be heard from five miles away.

- You can tell the age of a fish by the number of growth rings on each of its scales.

- Winters were colder a thousand years ago. In 1063 the River Thames froze for fourteen weeks.

- An iguana can hold its breath for 28 minutes.

- The so-called 'wild' horses of North America are actually feral animals – free-living descendants of domestic horses that escaped or were turned loose.

- The largest-known kidney stone weighed 1.36 kg.

- The most sensitive finger is the forefinger.

---------------- **SCIENCE AND NATURE** ----------------

- After a flash of lightning the sound of the thunder travels to you at about a mile every five seconds. This allows you to calculate how distant the storm is.

- It would be possible to boil 30 litres of water with the heat generated by the average adult human each day.

- An instrument developed at the University of Arizona by Dr Frank Low for taking temperature readings of distant planets was so sensitive it was capable of detecting a lit cigarette 10,000 miles (16,093 km) away.

- You are more likely to get stung by a bee in windy weather than in any other weather condition.

- The tongue is the only muscle in your body that is attached at only one end.

- From one giant redwood, or sequoia, it would be possible to build 60 average-sized houses. The trees can grow to over 300 ft (91 m) in height and 25 ft (7 m) in diameter.

- Humans are the only primates that do not have pigment in the palms of their hands.

SCIENCE AND NATURE

- The oldest-known goldfish lived to 41 years of age. Its name was Fred.

- The only breed of dog that has a black, rather than a pink, tongue is a chow.

- Surgeons perform better during operations if they are listening to music.

- When a chimpanzee's daubed prints were submitted in a test folio in Pretoria in place of a student's work, they were given a pass mark by the examiners.

- In a survey of 80,000 American women it was found that those who drank moderately had only half the heart-attack risk of those who didn't drink at all.

- The muscle with the longest name in the human body is the *levator labii superioris alaeque nasi* – one of the muscles of facial expression acting on the mouth and nose.

- A humpback whale's milk is 54% fat.

- Honeybees maintain a temperature of 94°F (34°C) in their hives all year round.

SCIENCE AND NATURE

- Nose prints are the most reliable way of identifying dogs.

- The longest recorded flight of a chicken was thirteen seconds.

- Compact discs read from the inside to the outside edge – the reverse of how a record works.

- A cat has 32 muscles in each ear.

- There are enough explosives on earth to annihilate mankind 50,000 times over.

- Spider monkeys like banana daiquiris.

- A human mucus membrane, which is used to smell, is the size of a first-class postage stamp.

- Identical twins do not have identical fingerprints.

- The human tooth has about 55 miles (89 km) of canals in it.

- Bees must visit some 5,000 flowers to make a single spoonful of honey.

SCIENCE AND NATURE

- According to a Gallup poll, 29% of people find the Christmas holidays more stressful than enjoyable.

- Every year the earth becomes about 12 tons (12,193 kg) heavier because of meteorites landing.

- When you sneeze all your bodily functions stop – including the heart.

- A pig's orgasm lasts for 30 minutes.

- The smallest fish in the world is the *Trimattum Nanus* of the *Chagos Archipelago*. It measures just 0.33 inches (0.8 cm) long.

- Cat's urine glows in black light.

- A 150-lb (68-kg) adult on earth would weigh 250 tons (254,013 kg) on the sun.

- Apples, not caffeine, are more efficient at waking you up in the morning.

- The blood of an octopus is pale blueish green.

- It takes only 7 lb (3 kg) of pressure to rip off your ear.

——————— SCIENCE AND NATURE ———————

- The human heart creates enough pressure to squirt blood 30 ft (9 m).

- Without an atmosphere the surface temperature on earth at the equator would be 80°C by day and fall to −140°C at night.

- Dogs like squeezy toys because they sound like animals in distress.

- So far man has survived on earth for two million years. The dinosaurs lasted 150 million years.

- The average computer user blinks seven times a minute.

- Extremely loud sounds, when properly directed, can actually bore holes through solid matter.

- After human death, post-mortem rigidity starts in the head, travels to the feet and leaves the same way it came – head to toe.

- A cat's jaws cannot move sideways.

- A UN survey revealed that postmen in Britain are bitten by dogs far less than in any other country.

SCIENCE AND NATURE

- It took a 19th-century Danish schoolmaster a lifetime to calculate pi to 800 decimal places. It took a modern computer only a few seconds to check his figures and find them correct.

- A hedgehog's heart beats 300 times a minute on average.

- A tiger's paw prints are called pug marks.

- Giraffes have no vocal cords.

- Emus have double-plumed feathers and they lay emerald/forest green eggs.

- A great horned owl can turn its head 270°.

- In the last 3,000 years no new animals have been domesticated.

- The pet ferret was domesticated more than 500 years before the house cat.

- A pig's skin is thickest on its back, where it can be up to ⅙ inch (0.4 cm) thick.

SCIENCE AND NATURE

- Calling a puppy to punish it teaches it not to come when it's called. It is best to reward a dog by bringing it to you – and to punish it by sending it away.

- Montana mountain goats butt heads so hard their hooves fall off.

- Societies in ancient Rome, Germany and China used urine as a mouthwash.

- Babies dream in the womb, according to medical experts.

- Two out of every five women in the US dye their hair.

- When you cross cattle with buffalo you get a beefalo.

- Dalmatian dogs are born pure white. Their spots don't appear until they are three or four days old.

- If you feed a seagull Alka Seltzer its stomach will explode.

- Skin temperature does not go much above 95°F (35°C) even on the hottest day.

- Mosquitoes are attracted to the colour blue more than twice as much as to any other single colour.

SCIENCE AND NATURE

- If the eggs spawned by all the female cod in one season survived they would fill the oceans from seabed to surface. Cod lay between four and five million eggs at a time – but usually only about five survive.

- Flying fish 'fly' at between 35 and 45 mph (56 and 72 kph).

- Thumbnails grow much more slowly than fingernails.

- A teaspoonful of neutron star material would weigh about 110 million tons (111,760,000 tonnes).

- Your hearing becomes less sharp after eating too much.

- Slugs travel at a top speed of .007 mph (.011 kph), can stretch to eleven times their length and have 27,000 teeth to help eat their food

- When the walkie-talkie was first introduced commercially, in 1934, it was described as a 'portable super-regenerative receiver and transmitter'.

- Sharks can detect the heartbeats of other fish.

- The tip of an elephant's trunk is so sensitive and flexible that it can pick up a pin.

SCIENCE AND NATURE

● Women suffer more tooth decay than men do.

● A female bed bug has survived 565 days without food.

● Most elephants weigh less than the tongue of the Blue Whale.

● An elephant can smell water 3 miles (5 km) away.

● Neither horses nor rabbits can vomit.

● The first Ford cars had Dodge engines.

● Water, which boils at 100°C at sea level, will boil at 70°C at the top of Mount Everest.

● Ingrown toenails are hereditary.

● A male emperor moth can smell a female up to 7 miles (11 km) away.

● A shark can detect one part of blood in 100 million parts of water.

● Armadillos have four babies at a time and they are always all the same sex.

SCIENCE AND NATURE

- A pelican can hold about 25 lb (11 kg) of fish in its pouch.

- The only insect that can turn its head is a praying mantis.

- In the Caribbean there are oysters that can climb trees.

- No one knows why a duck's quack doesn't echo.

- The common garden worm has five pairs of hearts.

- When *Voyager 2* visited Neptune it filmed a small, irregular white triangle that zips around Neptune's surface every sixteen hours or so and is now known as the Scooter.

- Each day 4 ½ lb (2 kg) of sunlight strike the earth.

- There are more beetles than any other creature in the world.

- It is illegal in Alaska to give a moose an alcoholic drink.

- When penguins hop on to an ice floe they always choose one that will take them back to land.

SCIENCE AND NATURE

- The lining of your digestive system is shed every three days.

- It is impossible to sneeze with your eyes open.

- The human brain stops growing at the age of eighteen.

- The only way to stop the pain of a flathead fish's sting is by rubbing its slime on the wound it gave you.

- The longest recorded life span of a camel was 35 years and five months.

- An elephant's trunk can hold four gallons of water.

- Solid hydrogen is the densest substance in the world at 70.6 g/cc.

- A bumblebee beats its wings 160 times a second.

- Every part of the hemlock plant is deadly poisonous – the flowers, leaves, roots, stems and seeds.

- Orcas kill sharks by torpedoing up into the shark's stomach from underneath, causing the shark to explode.

SCIENCE AND NATURE

- Each year the moon's orbit moves about 1.5 inches (3.8 cm) further away from the earth.

- If you were ejected into space, you would explode before you suffocated because there is no air pressure.

- The 2-ft-long (0.6-m) New Zealand mountain bird kea likes to eat the strips of rubber around car windows.

- Scientists working on the Manhattan Project in the early 1940s measured the time it took for an imploding shell of uranium to reach critical mass and initiate spontaneous fission in 'shakes of a lamb's tail'. One 'shake' equalled 1×10^{-8} s (one hundred millionth of a second). It took about three shakes of a lamb's tail.

- You can tell a turtle's gender by the noise it makes: males grunt, females hiss.

- Lady Coventry was an early victim of cosmetics. She died in October 1760 from the poisonous effects of regularly painting her face with white lead.

- The 1-oz brown bat, which is most common in North America, is capable of eating 500 insects an hour during its night-time feeding.

—————— **SCIENCE AND NATURE** ——————

● You burn more calories sleeping than watching television.

● Jellyfish are the wettest creatures on earth, being made up of 95.4% water. An average adult human has a water content of just over 60%.

● The only bone not connected to another bone in the human body is in the throat, at the back of the tongue.

● The oldest tortoise lived to the age of 152.

● Since 1600 a total of 109 species and subspecies of bird have become extinct.

● You can tell the sex of a crab by its stomach: the female's is beehive-shaped, while the male's is lighthouse-shaped.

● The largest-known mountain in the solar system is on Mars and is called Olympus Mons. It is a volcano three times the height of Everest.

● The sparrow was imported to New York in 1850 to cope with an excess of tree worms.

● The smallest unit of time is a yoctosecond.

-------------- **SCIENCE AND NATURE** --------------

- The 2.5-ton (2,540-kg), 55-ft-long (17-m) giant squid has the largest eyes of any animal on earth, each being more than a foot (0.3 m) in diameter.

- One way to tell seals and sea lions apart is that sea lions have external ears and testicles.

- For every extra kilogram carried on a space flight, 530 kg of extra fuel are need at lift-off.

- A normal dog has 42 teeth: 20 in the upper jaw and 22 in the lower jaw. A human adult has 32 teeth equally divided between the two jaws.

- A fully mature oak tree sheds about 700,000 leaves every year.

- As of 2002 in New York City rats outnumbered humans by twelve to one.

- The only time in history when the roman numerals in a year were written using all the numerals in order from highest value to lowest value was 1666 – MDCLXVI (1,000 plus 500 plus 100 plus 50 plus 10 plus 5 plus 1).

—————— **SCIENCE AND NATURE** ——————

- There are 62,000 miles (99,777 km) of arteries, veins and blood capillaries in the human body.

- In Hong Kong a red-and-white-striped pole outside a premises may not necessarily indicate a barber's shop. It is also the sign for a brothel.

- A cubic mile of sea water contains, on average, more than £60 million worth of gold and £6 million worth of silver.

- The skin that peels off after sunburn is called blype.

- In a dental experiment on elephants, motor-car tyres were chopped up and baked in their bread. The elephants never noticed.

- You can avoid sinking in quicksand by lying on your back and raising your legs slowly.

- The northern fur seal has more mates each year than any other mammal. The average male will mate with between 40 and 60 females each season.

- In 1976 the swine flu vaccine caused more deaths than the illness it was intended to prevent.

SCIENCE AND NATURE

- A chicken is the only animal that can be eaten before it is born and after it is dead.

- If you were locked in a completely sealed room you would die of carbon dioxide poisoning before oxygen deprivation.

- Ants cannot chew their food; they move their jaws sideways like scissors to extract juices from it.

- Peanuts are one of the ingredients of dynamite.

- Your thumb is the same length as your nose.

- Honeybees have hair on their eyes.

- Very tall buildings naturally lean towards the course of the sun.

- Most spiders have eight eyes.

- Cats have more than 100 vocal sounds, while dogs only have about ten.

- Spiders do not get caught in their own webs because they cover themselves with a greasy anti-silk film.

SCIENCE AND NATURE

- Some female hyenas have a pseudo penis.

- A South American termite queen can produce 30,000 eggs in a day and do this daily for up to a year. A colony of more than five million termites can come from a single queen.

- The longest recorded lifespan of a slug is eighteen months.

- The world's elephants could drink dry the Serpentine lake in Hyde Park, London, if they all supped at the same time.

- When press tycoon William Randolph Hearst sent a telegram to a leading astronomer asking if there was life on Mars and to please cable 1,000 words on the subject, he received the reply: 'Nobody knows' repeated 500 times.

- The difference between fowl and poultry is that poultry are domesticated fowl.

- In Australia the male antechinus mouse has up to sixteen partners a time in sex sessions in trees lasting up to twelve hours. Often they become so weak they fall out of the trees and are killed.

---------- **SCIENCE AND NATURE** ----------

- The storage capacity of a human brain exceeds 4 terrabytes.

- There are 45 miles (72 km) of nerves in the human body.

- A sow will always have an even number of teats or nipples – usually twelve.

- The heaviest organs in the human body are the lungs, which together weigh about 42 oz (approx. 1,176 g).

- Hamsters love to eat crickets.

- A cross between a greyhound and a terrier is a whippet.

- Lycanthropy is a disease in which a man thinks he's a wolf. It is the scientific name for wolfman or werewolf.

- You lose enough dead skin cells in your lifetime to fill eight 5-lb (2 kg) flour bags.

- Babies are born without kneecaps. They do not appear until the child reaches two to six years of age.

- Insects in India each year eat more food than the entire human population of London.

SCIENCE AND NATURE

- The world's termites outweigh the world's humans by 10 to 1.

- The female praying mantis is such a deadly hunter that she often eats her partner immediately after mating. Sometimes she begins her meal while they are still copulating.

- Shrews and platypuses are the only mammals that are poisonous.

- Butterflies taste with their feet.

- The world's smallest mammal is the bumblebee bat of Thailand, weighing less than a penny.

- A sneeze travels out of your mouth at over 100 mph (161 kph).

- An average adult human being has around 2,381,248 sweat glands on their skin.

- The average talker sprays about 300 microscopic saliva drops per minute – about 2.5 droplets per word.

——————— **SCIENCE AND NATURE** ———————

- On take-off an *Apollo* spacecraft develops more power than all the cars in Britain put together.

- So important to human dexterity is the thumb that the brain devotes a larger portion to controlling it than to controlling the chest and abdomen.

- There are 450 hairs in an average eyebrow.

- Studies show that if a cat falls off the seventh floor of a building it has about a 30% less chance of surviving than a cat that falls off the twentieth floor. It takes about eight floors for the cat to realise what is happening, relax and correct itself.

- In 1977 a thirteen-year-old child found a tooth growing out of his left foot.

- Every night the parrot fish sleeps inside a mucus cocoon, which it constructs daily to block its body smell from predators.

- Most hamsters blink one eye at a time.

- Your right lung takes in more air than your left lung.

---------- **SCIENCE AND NATURE** ----------

- Human birth-control pills work on gorillas.

- The underside of a horse's hoof is called a frog. The frog peels off several times a year to be replaced by a new growth.

- A dragonfly has a lifespan of just 24 hours.

- Baby robins eat 14 ft (4 m) of earthworms a day.

- Pearls melt in vinegar.

- In his book *The Insects* naturalist Url N Lanham reports that the aphid reproduction cycle is so rapid that the females are born pregnant.

- Even with its favourite food laid out to tempt it, a giant tortoise can manage a top speed of only five yards (4.5 m) a minute – 0.17 mph (0.2 kph).

- The honey badger can withstand hundreds of African bee stings that would kill any other animal.

- It would take seven billion particles of fog to fill a teaspoon.

- You blink over ten million times a year.

—————— **SCIENCE AND NATURE** ——————

- Alligators cannot move backwards.

- A rat can chew through just about any building material, including concrete.

- A pig always sleeps on its right side.

- When opossums are playing 'possum' they are not playing but have passed out from sheer terror.

- If you divide the Great Pyramid's perimeter by twice its height you get pi to the fifteenth digit.

- The rattlesnake has the best heat-detecting equipment in nature. Using the two organs between its eyes and nostrils it can locate a mouse by its body heat at a distance of 15 m.

- The archerfish brings down its insect prey with well-aimed mouthfuls of spit. It is even able to compensate for refraction when it shoots from under water.

- Moths hear through the hairs on their bodies.

- Over a thousand birds a year die from smashing into windows.

—————— **SCIENCE AND NATURE** ——————

- A robin's egg is blue, but if you put it in vinegar for 30 days it turns yellow.

- A baby platypus remains blind after birth for 11 weeks.

- A barnacle has the largest penis of any other animal in relation to its size.

- A camel's backbone is just as straight as a horse's.

- A chameleon's tongue is twice the length of its body.

- A donkey will sink in quicksand but a mule won't.

- A dragonfly has a lifespan of four to seven weeks.

- A duck has three eyelids.

- A female ferret will die if it goes on heat and cannot find a mate.

- A geep is a cross between a goat and a sheep.

- A group of frogs is called an army.

- A group of goats is called a trip.

SCIENCE AND NATURE

- A group of hares is called a husk.

- A group of kangaroos is called a mob.

- A group of owls is called a parliament.

- A group of rhinos is called a crash.

- A group of toads is called a knot.

- A hedgehog's heart beats 300 times a minute on average.

- A jackrabbit can jump as high as 15 feet.

- A large swarm of locusts can eat 80,000 tons of corn in a day.

- A male chimpanzee is five times hornier than the average human.

- A mole can dig over 250 feet of tunnel in a single night.

- A rat can last longer without water than a camel.

—————— **SCIENCE AND NATURE** ——————

- A rodent's teeth never stop growing. They are worn down by the animal's constant gnawing on bark, leaves and other vegetables.

- A scallop has a total of 35 eyes which are all blue.

- A sheep, a duck and a rooster were the first passengers in a hot air balloon.

- A single sheep's fleece might well contain as many as 26 million fibres.

- A species of Australian dragonfly has been clocked at 36mph.

- A species of earthworm in Australia grows up to 10 feet in length.

- A square mile of fertile earth has 32 million earthworms in it.

- A strand from the web of the golden spider is as strong as a steel wire of the same size.

SCIENCE AND NATURE

- According to Dr David Gems, a British geneticist, sex-craved male mice, who spend five to 11 hours per day pursuing female mice, could live years longer if they abstained.

- After eating, the housefly regurgitates its food and eats it again.

- All porcupines float in water.

- Alligators cannot move backwards.

- An estimated 80 per cent of creatures on earth have six legs.

- An octopus will eat its own arms if it gets really hungry.

- An ostrich's eye is bigger than its brain.

- Apart from humans, certain species of chimpanzee are the only animals to experiment sexually. They have been known to 'wife swap' and indulge in group sex.

- Basilisks are frequently called Jesus Christ Lizards because of their ability to run on water.

—————— SCIENCE AND NATURE ——————

- Bats always turn left when exiting a cave.

- Bats can live up to 30 years or more.

- Bees do not have ears.

- Between 1902 and 1907 the same tiger killed 436 people in India.

- Butterflies taste with their hind feet.

- Carnivorous animals will not eat another animal that has been hit by a lightning strike.

- Cats have over 100 vocal sounds, while dogs only have about 10.

- A cockroach's favourite food is the glue on the back of stamps.

- During its lifetime an oyster changes its sex from male to female and back several times.

- Every single hamster in the US today comes from a single litter captured in Syria in 1930.

--- **SCIENCE AND NATURE** ---

● Flamingos are pink because they consume vast quantities of algae.

● Flamingos can live up to 80 years.

● Flamingos can only eat with their heads upside down.

● Frog-eating bats identify edible from poisonous frogs by listening to the mating calls of male frogs. Frogs counter by hiding and using short, difficult to locate calls.

● Frogs must close their eyes to swallow.

● Giant squids have eyes as big as watermelons.

● Giant tortoises can live to be 150 years old or older.

● Gorillas often sleep for up to 14 hours a day.

● Herons have been observed to drop insects on the water and then catch the fish that surface for the bugs.

● Hippopotami cannot swim.

● If a frog's mouth is held open for too long the frog will suffocate.

SCIENCE AND NATURE

- Iguanas, koalas and Komodo dragons all have two penises.

- In 1859, 24 rabbits were released in Australia. Within six years the population grew to two million.

- In Miami, Florida, roosting vultures have taken to snatching poodles from rooftop patios.

- It is estimated that millions of trees are planted by forgetful squirrels.

- It was discovered on a space mission that a frog can throw up. The frog throws up its stomach first, so the stomach is dangling out of its mouth. Then the frog uses its forearms to dig out all of the stomach's contents and then swallows the stomach back down.

- It is physically impossible for pigs to look up in the sky.

- Jackals have one more pair of chromosomes than dogs or wolves.

- Jackrabbits can reach a speed of 50 miles per hour and can leap as high as five feet.

- Jaguars are scared of dogs.

SCIENCE AND NATURE

- Japan is the largest exporter of frogs' legs.

- Lorne Green had one of his nipples bitten off by an alligator while host of *Lorne Green's Wild Kingdom*.

- Male bees will try to attract sex partners with orchid fragrance.

- Man and the two-toed sloth are the only land animals that typically mate face to face.

- Many hamsters only blink one eye at a time.

- Mexican free-tailed bats sometimes fly up to two miles high to feed or to catch tail-winds that carry them over long distances at speeds of more than 60 miles per hour.

- Mice will nurse babies that are not their own.

- Mice, whales, elephants, giraffes and man all have seven neck vertebrae.

- Moose have very poor vision. Some have even tried to mate with cars.

—— SCIENCE AND NATURE ——

- Mongooses were brought to Hawaii to kill rats. This plan failed because rats are nocturnal while the mongoose hunts during the day.

- Most published species of dinosaurs have been published within the last 20 years.

- Next to man, the porpoise is the most intelligent creature on earth.

- Orangutans warn people to stay out of their territory by belching.

- Porcupines are excellent swimmers, because their quills are hollow.

- Rats can't vomit.

- Rhinos are in the same family as horses, and are thought to have inspired the myth of the unicorn.

- Seals must teach their young how to swim.

- Slugs have four noses.

- Some dinosaurs were as small as hens.

SCIENCE AND NATURE

- Southern Indian drug addicts get high by having venomous snakes bite their tongues. This can give addicts a 16-hour high, but can be very deadly.

- Tarantulas do not use muscles to move their legs. They control the amount of blood pumped into them to extend and retract their legs.

- The beautiful but deadly Australian sea wasp (Chironex fleckeri) is the most venomous jellyfish in the world. Its cardio toxic venom has caused the deaths of 66 people off the coast of Queensland since 1880, with victims dying within one to three minutes if medical aid is not available.

- The adult electric eel has enough electrical power in it to power a house of about 1,200 square feet.

- The cheetah can reach a speed of up to 45 miles per hour in only two seconds.

- The colour of a yak's milk is pink.

- The deepest penguin dive was 1261ft under the water.

- The electric eel has an average discharge of 400 volts.

SCIENCE AND NATURE

- The elephant is the only mammal that can't jump.

- The giant cricket of Africa enjoys eating human hair.

- The honey badger can withstand hundreds of African bee stings that would kill any other animal.

- The Kansas City Railroad used to stop their trains, in 1868, to allow the passengers to shoot at passing buffalo.

- The leg bones of a bat are so thin that no bat can walk.

- The longest species of earthworm is the Megascolides australis, found in Australia in 1868. An average specimen measures 4 feet in length, 2 feet when contracted, and 7 feet when naturally extended.

- The lifespan of a squirrel is about nine years.

- The male gypsy moth can smell the virgin female gypsy moth from eight miles away.

- The Nile and Indo-Pacific saltwater crocodiles are the only two crocodiles that are considered true man-eaters.

- The octopus's testicles are located in its head.

———— SCIENCE AND NATURE ————

- The only continent without reptiles or snakes is Antarctica.

- The original name for butterfly was the flutterby.

- The poison arrow frog has enough poison to kill about 2,200 people.

- The poisonous copperhead smells like fresh cut cucumbers.

- The Portuguese Man-of-War 'jellyfish' tentacles have been known to grow a mile in length, catching anything in its path by stinging its prey.

- The pupil of an octopus's eye is rectangular.

- The Quahog clam is the longest living animal, with a maximum age of up to 200 years old.

- The Queen (or more precisely the Royal Household) owns all swans in England. The post of Royal Swankeeper is a post that has been around since 1215 and he and his staff are responsible for keeping accurate statistics about the number and whereabouts of the royal swans.

SCIENCE AND NATURE

- The scientific name for a gorilla is 'gorilla gorilla gorilla'.

- The shrimp's heart is in its head.

- The tuatara lizard of New Zealand has three eyes – two in the centre of its head and one on top.

- The tuatara's metabolism is so slow they only have to breathe once an hour.

- The typical laboratory mouse runs five miles per night on its treadmill.

- The Weddell seal can travel under water for seven miles without surfacing for air.

- The woolly mammoth, extinct since the Ice Age, had tusks almost 16 feet long.

- The word alligator comes from 'El Lagarto' which is Spanish for 'The Lizard.'

- The world camel population is 19,627,000.

- There have been over 1,500 documented sightings of Bigfoot since 1958.

SCIENCE AND NATURE

- There is no record of a non-rabid wolf attack on a human.

- Tigers have striped skin, not just striped fur.

- To escape the grip of a crocodile's jaws, push your thumbs into its eyeballs – it will let you go instantly.

- To keep cool, ostriches urinate on their legs; it then evaporates like sweat.

- To see at night as well as an owl, you would need eyeballs as big as a grapefruit.

- When cornered, the horned toad shoots blood from its eyes.

- Woodpecker scalps, porpoise teeth and giraffe tails have all been used as money.

- Worldwide, bats are the most important natural enemies of night-flying insects.

- You can cut up a starfish into pieces and each piece will grow into a completely new starfish. .

—— SCIENCE AND NATURE ——

● Polar bears have more problems with overheating than they do with cold. Even in very cold weather, they quickly overheat when they try to run.

● Camel's milk does not curdle.

● Camels have three eyelids to protect their eyes from blowing sand.

● Despite its reputation for being finicky, the average cat consumes about 127,750 calories a year, nearly 28 times its own weight in food and the same amount again in liquids. In case you were wondering, cats cannot survive on a vegetarian diet.

● It is estimated that a single toad may catch and eat as many as 10,000 insects in the course of a summer.

● It is the female lion who does more than 90 per cent of the hunting, while the male is afraid to risk his life, or simply prefers to rest.

● Dinosaurs were among the most sophisticated animals that ever lived on earth. They survived for nearly 150 million years – 75 times longer than humans have now lived on earth.

SCIENCE AND NATURE

- Disc-winged bats of Latin America have adhesive discs on both wings and feet that enable them to live in unfurling banana leaves (or even walk up a window pane!).

- It takes 24 hours for a tiny newborn swan to peck its way out of its shell.

- A 42-foot sperm whale has about seven tons of oil in it.

- A baby blue whale is 25 feet long at birth.

- A baby caribou is so swift it can easily outrun its mother when it is only three days old.

- A baby giraffe is about six feet tall at birth.

- It takes a lobster approximately seven years to grow to be one pound

- A baby grey whale drinks enough milk to fill more than 2,000 bottles a day.

- It takes about 50 hours for a snake to digest one frog.

- It takes an average of 345 squirts to yield a gallon of milk from a cow's udder.

———————— **SCIENCE AND NATURE** ————————

- It takes approximately 69,000 venom extractions from the coral snake to fill a one-pint container.

- Dolphins do not breathe automatically, as humans do, and so they do not sleep as humans do. If they become unconscious, they would sink to the bottom of the sea. Without the oxygen they need to take in periodically, they would die.

- Dolphins have killed sharks by ramming them with their snouts.

- Dolphins jump out of the water to conserve energy. It is easier to move through the air than through the water.

- Dolphins swim in circles while they sleep with the eye on the outside of the circle open to keep watch for predators. After a certain amount of time, they reverse and swim in the opposite direction with the opposite eye open.

- Jackrabbits are powerful jumpers. A 20-inch adult can leap 20 feet in a single bound.

SCIENCE AND NATURE

- Due to a retinal adaptation that reflects light back to the retina, the night vision of tigers is six times better than that of humans.

- During the 1800s, swan skins were used to make European ladies' powder puffs and swan feathers were used to adorn fashionable hats.

- Rats can swim for a half mile without resting, and they can tread water for three days straight.

- Rattlesnakes gather in groups to sleep through the winter. Sometimes up to 1,000 of them will coil up together to keep warm.

- Kangaroo rats never drink water. Like their relatives the pocket mice, they carry their own water source within them, producing fluids from the food they eat and the air they breathe.

- Reindeer have scent glands between their hind toes. The glands help them leave scent trails for the herd. Researchers say the odour smells cheesy.

- Just like people, mother chimpanzees often develop lifelong relationships with their offspring.

SCIENCE AND NATURE

- Kangaroos can move as fast as 30 miles per hour and can leap up to 25 feet in the air.

- Kangaroos usually give birth to one young annually. The young kangaroo, or joey, is born alive at a very immature stage, when it is only about 2cm long and weighs less than a gram.

- Reptiles are never slimy. Their scales have few glands, and are usually silky to the touch.

- Each eye of the chameleon is independent of the other. The lizard can watch and study two totally different pictures at the same time.

- Kittens are born both blind and deaf, but the vibration of their mother's purring is a physical signal that the kittens can feel – it acts like a homing device, signalling them to nurse.

- Kittens can clock an amazing 31 miles per hour at full speed, and can cover about three times their body length per leap.

- Eagles mate while airborne.

SCIENCE AND NATURE

- Koalas and humans are the only animals with unique prints. Koala prints cannot be distinguished from human fingerprints.

- Earlier penguins were capable of flight.

- Rome has more homeless cats per square mile than any other city in the world.

- Komodo dragons eat deer and wild boar.

- Lanolin, an essential ingredient of many expensive cosmetics, is, in its native form, a foul-smelling, waxy, tarlike substance extracted from the fleece of sheep.

- Running in short bursts, the cheetah can reach a speed of 62 miles per hour (100 kilometres per hour).

- Elephants and short-tailed shrews get by on only two hours of sleep a day.

- Elephants communicate in sound waves below the frequency that humans can hear.

SCIENCE AND NATURE

● Scientific researchers say promiscuous species of monkeys appear to have stronger immune systems than less sexually active ones.

● Elephants have been known to remain standing after they die.

● Elephants perform greeting ceremonies when a member of the group returns after a long time away. The welcoming animals spin around, flap their ears and trumpet.

● Scientists still know very little about the giant squid, except what can be gleaned from the carcasses of about 100 beached squid dating back to 1639. Despite centuries of myths and exciting tales of sightings of giant squid, more information is known about dinosaurs.

● Lions sleep up to 20 hours a day.

● Sea otters have the world's densest fur – a million hairs per square inch.

● Sea otters inhabit water but never get wet because they have two coats of fur.

SCIENCE AND NATURE

- Sea sponges are used in drugs for treating asthma and cancer.

- Lobsters moult 20 to 30 times before reaching the one-pound market size.

- Seals and whales keep warm in the icy polar water thanks to a layer of fat called blubber under their skin. Whale blubber can reach up to 20 inches (50 centimetres) thick.

- Seals can sleep under water and surface for air without even waking.

- Seals can withstand water pressure of up to 850 pounds per square inch.

- Seals have back flippers that can't bend under the body in order to walk on land, while sea lions use their leg-like hind flippers to 'walk' on land.

- Male boars form harems.

- Sharks can be dangerous even before they are born. Scientist Stewart Springer was bitten by a sand tiger shark embryo while he was examining its pregnant mother.

SCIENCE AND NATURE

- Male cockatoos can be taught to speak, but females can only chirp and sing.

- Sharks can travel up to 40 miles per hour.

- Sharks' fossil records date back more than twice as long as that of the dinosaurs.

- Male monkeys lose the hair on their heads in the same manner men do.

- Male sea lions may have more than 100 wives and sometimes go three months without eating.

- Shrimp swim backwards.

- The dodo, extinct less than 100 years after being discovered by the Dutch in 1598, was not a prolific species. The female laid just one egg a year.

- The dog and the turkey were the only two domesticated animals in ancient Mexico.

- The domestic cat is the only species able to hold its tail vertically while walking. Wild cats hold their tail horizontally, or tucked between their legs while walking.

SCIENCE AND NATURE

- Sidewinders are snakes that move by looping their bodies up in the air and pushing against the ground when they land. Their tracks in the ground would look like a series of straight lines angling in the direction the snake was travelling.

- The duckbill platypus of Australia can store up to 600 worms in its large cheek pouches.

- The Egyptian vulture, a white bird about the size of a raven, throws stones with its beak to open ostrich eggs to eat. This bird is one of the very few animals that, like man, manipulates objects as tools.

- Skunks have more than smell to protect themselves. They can withstand five times the snake venom that would kill a rabbit.

- Many types of fish – called mouthbrooders – carry their eggs in their mouths until the babies hatch and can care for themselves.

- Snakes do not have eyelids, so even when they're asleep they cannot close their eyes. They do have a protective layer of clear scales, called brille, over their eyes.

--------------- **SCIENCE AND NATURE** ---------------

- The electric eel is the most shocking animal on earth –
  no other animal packs such a big charge. If attacking a
  large prey, a nine-foot-long eel can discharge about 800
  volts. One zap could stun a human. The larger the eel,
  the bigger the charge.

- So that it can pull its lithe body into a tight, prickly little
  ball for defence, the hedgehog has a large muscle running
  along its stomach.

- The electric organs in an electric eel make up four-fifths
  of its body.

- Deer like to eat marijuana.

- Some bullfrogs pretend to be dead when captured, but
  quickly hop away when let go.

- The emperor penguin is the largest type of penguin. It is
  also the deepest diver, reaching depths of 870 feet
  (260 metres) and staying there for up to 18 minutes.

- Mice, whales, elephants, giraffes and humans all have
  seven neck vertebra.

SCIENCE AND NATURE

- The emu is Australia's largest bird at a height of seven feet tall. It can't fly, but it can swim and has the ability to run up to 40 miles per hour.

- Some sharks swim in a figure eight when frightened.

- Milk snakes lay about 13 eggs – in piles of animal manure.

- The enormous livers of basking sharks, which can account for up to one-third of their body weight, produce a valuable oil used to lubricate engines and manufacture cosmetics.

- More people are killed in Africa by crocodiles than by lions.

- Some mantis shrimp travel by doing backward somersaults.

- More species of fish live in a single tributary of the Amazon River than in all the rivers in North America combined.

- The European eagle owl is the largest owl in the world. It can measure 28 inches (70 centimetres) tall with a wingspan of five feet (150 centimetres) wide.

———— **SCIENCE AND NATURE** ————

- More than two million southern fur seals – 95 per cent of the world's population – crowd onto the shores of South Georgia Island each summer. Half the world's population of southern elephant seals also come to the island to mate.

- The eyes and nose of a frog are on top of its head, enabling it to breathe and see when most of its body is under the water.

- Spider silk is an extremely strong material and its on-weight basis has been proven to be stronger than steel. Experts suggest that a pencil-thick strand of silk could stop a Boeing 747 in flight.

- South America's harpy eagles eat monkeys. The birds build twig platforms in the treetops where they lay their eggs.

- The fastest bird in the world is the Asian spine-tailed swift. In a level flight, it can reach a speed of 102 miles per hour (170 kilometres per hour).

- Squirrels can climb trees faster than they can run on the ground.

SCIENCE AND NATURE

- Starbuck, a Canadian bull who sired 200,000 dairy cows and an equal number of bulls in his life, earned an estimated $25 million before he died in 1998. After his death, his frozen semen was still selling for $250 a dose.

- The killer whale, or orca, is the fastest sea mammal. It can reach speeds up to 34 miles per hour (56 kilometres per hour) in pursuit of prey.

- The killer whale, or orca, is not a whale but the largest member of the dolphin family.

- The female blue crab can lay up to one million eggs in a day.

- The female condor lays a single egg once every two years.

- Jellyfish are comprised of more than 95 per cent water and have no brain, heart or bones, and no actual eyes.

- Studies show that the breeds of dogs that bite the least are, in order: the Golden Retriever, Labrador Retriever, Shetland Sheepdog, Old English Sheepdog and the Welsh Terrier.

——————— SCIENCE AND NATURE ———————

- Sue, the world's largest, most complete, and best preserved Tyrannosaurus Rex, made her grand debut to the public on 17 May 2000, at the Field Museum in Chicago, Illinois.

- The female knot-tying weaverbird will refuse to mate with a male who has built a shoddy nest. If spurned, the male must take the nest apart and completely rebuild it in order to win the affections of the female.

- Surviving all dangers, a wild cobra may live up to 20 years.

- The female pigeon cannot lay eggs if she is alone. In order for her ovaries to function, she must be able to see another pigeon. If no other pigeon is available, her own reflection in a mirror will suffice.

- The kiwi, national bird of New Zealand, can't fly. It lives in a hole in the ground, is almost blind and lays only one egg each year. Despite this, it has survived for more than 70 million years.

- The two best known cat noises are roaring and purring. Only four species can roar, and they don't purr: lions, leopards, tigers and jaguars.

——————— SCIENCE AND NATURE ———————

- The Kodiak grizzly bear is the world's largest meat-eating animal living on land. The Kodiak can weigh up to 500 pounds more than any other kind of bear.

- The 20 million Mexican free-tail bats from Bracken Cave, Texas, eat approximately 200 tons of insects nightly.

- The largest bird egg in the world today is that of the ostrich. Ostrich eggs are from six to eight inches long. Because of their size and the thickness of their shells, they take 40 minutes to hard-boil.

- The largest great white shark ever caught measured 37 feet and weighed 24,000 pounds. It was found in a herring weir in New Brunswick in 1930.

- The harmless whale shark holds the title of largest fish, with the record being a 59-footer captured in Thailand in 1919.

- The first dinosaur to be found and recognized as a huge reptile was the Megalosaurus. This dinosaur was a meat eater.

- The African eagle, swooping at more than 100 miles per hour, can brake to a halt in 20 feet.

SCIENCE AND NATURE

- The aardvark has such a well-developed sense of hearing, it can detect and locate distant ants on a nighttime march.

- The first dinosaur to be given a name was the Iguanodon, found in Sussex, United Kingdom, in 1823. It was not the first dinosaur to be found.

- The first flying animals were the pterosaurs that appeared over 200 million years ago. They were closer to flying reptiles than birds.

- The African lungfish can live without water for up to four years. When a drought occurs, it digs a pit and encloses itself in a capsule of slime and earth, leaving a small opening for breathing. The capsule dries and hardens, but the fish is protected. When rain comes, the capsule dissolves and the lungfish swims away.

- The largest known egg ever laid by a creature was that of the extinct Aepyornis of Madagascar. The egg was 9.5 inches long. It had a volume of 2.35 gallons.

- The first medical use of leeches dates back to approximately 2,500 years ago. The leech's saliva contains a property that acts as an anticoagulant for human blood.

SCIENCE AND NATURE

- The largest order of mammals, with about 1,700 species, is rodents. Bats are second with about 950 species.

- The five fastest birds are: the peregrine falcon that can fly up to 175mph hour, the spine-tailed swift that can go 106mph, the frigate bird at 95mph, the spur-winged goose at 88mph, and the red-breasted merganser at 80mph.

- The albatross can glide on air currents for several days and can even sleep while in flight.

- The albatross drinks sea water. It has a special desalinization apparatus that strains out and excretes all excess salt.

- The last wolf in Great Britain was killed in Scotland, in 1743. Wolves were extinct in England by 1500.

- The leech has 32 brains.

- The leech will gorge itself up to five times its body weight and then just fall off its victim.

- The flying fish builds up speed in the water then leaps into the air to escape predators. Once in the air, it can stay airborne for up to 325 feet (100m).

--------------- **SCIENCE AND NATURE** ---------------

- The flying snake of Java and Malaysia is able to flatten itself out like a ribbon and sail like a glider from tree to tree.

- The gait of the giraffe is a pace, with both legs on one side moving together. Because of its long stride, a giraffe is quicker than it appears. The animal, at full gallop, can run about 30 miles per hour.

- The Asiatic elephant takes 608 days to give birth, or just over 20 months.

- The anaconda, one of the world's largest snakes, gives birth to its young instead of laying eggs.

- The lethal Lion's Mane jellyfish has a bell reaching up to eight feet in diameter, and tentacles longer than a blue whale – up to 200 feet long. Juveniles are pink, turning red as they mature, and then becoming brownish purple when adults.

- The gastric juices of a snake can digest bones and teeth – but not fur or hair.

- The anteater hasn't any teeth or jaws. Its sticky tongue measures over a foot long.

--------- **SCIENCE AND NATURE** ---------

- The gecko lizard can run on the ceiling without falling because its toes have flaps of skin that act like suction cups.

- The longest lizard in the world is the Komodo dragon at 10 feet long. Next are the water monitor at 8.8 feet, then the perenty at 7.8 feet, the common iguana at five feet and the marine iguana at five feet.

- The loudest bird in the world is the male bellbird, found in Central and South America. To attract mates, the male makes a clanging sound like a bell that can be heard from miles away.

- The armour of the armadillo is not as tough as it appears. It is very pliable, much like a human fingernail.

- The male fox will mate for life and, if the female dies, he remains single for the rest of his life. However, if the male dies, the female will hook up with a new mate.

- The male house wren builds several nests as part of his courtship ritual. Once the nests are completed, his potential bride looks them all over, then selects one as her preferred choice for the laying of her eggs.

SCIENCE AND NATURE

- The giant Pacific octopus can fit its entire body through an opening no bigger than the size of its beak.

- The giant squid is the largest creature without a backbone. It weighs up to 2.5 tons and grows up to 55 feet long. Each eye is a foot or more in diameter.

- The giraffe's heart is huge; it weighs 25 pounds, is two feet long and has walls up to three inches thick.

- The girth of the Gila monster lizard's tail may shrink by 80 per cent during times of low food supply.

- The glue of a barnacle cannot be dissolved with strong acids or temperatures set as high as 440°F.

- There are more caribou in Alaska than people.

- The most carnivorous of all bears is the polar bear. Its diet consists almost entirely of seals and fish.

- The most venomous of all snakes, the Inland Taipan, has enough venom in one bite to kill more than 200,000 mice.

SCIENCE AND NATURE

- The grey wolf is the largest wild dog alive today. As an adult a grey wolf can weigh up to 176 pounds (80 kilograms).

- There are more than 150 breeds of horses in the world.

- The great horned owl can turn its head 270 degrees.

- There are no wild deer of any kind in Australia, and the small red deer is the only one found in Africa.

- The mudskipper is a fish that can actually walk on land.

- There are no penguins at the North Pole. In fact, there are no penguins anywhere in the Northern Hemisphere (outside of zoos). All 17 varieties of the bird are found below the equator, primarily in Antarctica.

- The grizzly bear is capable of running as fast as the average horse.

- There are seven species of bears: the American black bear, the Asian black bear, the brown bear, the polar bear, the sloth bear, the spectacled bear and the sun bear.

———— SCIENCE AND NATURE ————

- The nest of the bald eagle can weigh well over a ton.

- There are some 50 different species of sea snakes, and all of them are venomous. They thrive in abundance along the coast from the Persian Gulf to Japan and around Australia and Melanesia. Their venom is 10 times as virulent as that of the cobra. Humans bitten by them have died within two-and-a-half hours.

- The New Guinea singing dog's most unique characteristic is its dramatic ability to vary the pitch of its howl. The animal does not bark repetitively but has a complex vocal behaviour, including yelps, whines and single-note howls.

- There are species of mice that live in marshy places and are excellent swimmers.

- The Nile crocodile averages about 45 years in the wild, and may live up to 80 years in captivity.

- The normal body temperature of the Clydesdale horse is 101°F (38°C).

SCIENCE AND NATURE

- The hare can travel up to 45 miles per hour, whereas the rabbit can achieve an average speed of just 35 miles per hour.

- The heaviest bird in the world is the Kori bustard. The Kori weighs around 31 pounds (14 kilograms) on average, but the largest one found was over 40 pounds (18 kilograms).

- The heaviest flighted birds in the world are the great bustard at 40 pounds, the trumpeter swan at 37 pounds, the mute swan at 36 pounds, the albatross at 34 pounds and the whooper swan at 34 pounds.

- There is a strong bond between mother and child among orangutans. Orangutan infants cling almost continually to their mothers until they are one years old.

- The hides of mature female blue sharks are more than twice as thick as those of males, probably as a protection against courtship bites.

- The hippopotamus gives birth under water and nurses its young in the river as well, although the young hippos must come up periodically for air.

SCIENCE AND NATURE

- There is just one known species of ostrich in the world – it is in the order of Struthioniformes.

- There is no mention of cats or rats in the Bible.

- There is no single cat called the panther. The name is commonly applied to the leopard, but it is also used to refer to the puma and the jaguar. A black panther is really a black leopard.

- The odour of a skunk can be detected by a human a mile away.

- The only country in the world that has a Bill of Rights for cows is India.

- There were about 60 million bison when the Europeans landed in America. By the 1880s, all but 500 bison were killed. Today there are 350,000 bison in America.

- The only dog to ever appear in a Shakespearean play was Crab in *The Two Gentlemen of Verona*.

- Thinking that a giraffe's parents were a camel and a leopard, the Europeans once called the animal a 'camelopard'.

SCIENCE AND NATURE

- The optimum depth of water in a birdbath is two-and-a-half inches. Less water makes it difficult for birds to take a bath; more makes them afraid.

- The onomatopoeia for a dog's bark in Japanese is wan-wan.

- The horned owl is not horned. Two tufts of feathers were mistaken for horns.

- The horned lizard of the American southwest may squirt a thin stream of blood from the corners of its eyes when frightened.

- Thoroughbred horses are so thin-skinned their veins are visible beneath the skin, especially on the legs.

- Though human noses have an impressive five million olfactory cells with which to smell, sheepdogs have 220 million, enabling them to smell 44 times better than man.

- The howler monkey is the loudest animal living in the rainforests of South America. Their voices can be heard up to five miles (eight kilometres) away.

——— SCIENCE AND NATURE ———

- The ostrich has only two toes, unlike most birds, which have three or four.

- The hum of a hummingbird comes from the super-fast beat of the wings. The smallest ones beat their wings the fastest – up to 80 times per second. Even the slower beat of bigger hummingbirds' wings (20 times per second) is so fast you can only see a blur.

- Tiger cubs are born blind and weigh only about two to three pounds (1kg), depending on the subspecies. They live on milk for six to eight weeks before the female begins taking them to kills to feed. Tigers have fully developed canines by 16 months of age, but they do not begin making their own kills until about 18 months of age.

- The owl is the only bird to drop its upper eyelid to wink. All other birds raise their lower eyelids.

- The hummingbird is the only bird that can fly backwards.

- Tigers have stripes to help them hide in the rainforest undergrowth. The black and gold stripes break up the outline of the tiger's body making it very hard to see.

-------------- **SCIENCE AND NATURE** --------------

- The owl parrot can't fly, and builds its nest under tree roots.

- The hummingbird's tiny brain, 4.2 per cent of its body weight, is proportionately the largest in the bird kingdom.

- To be called a mammal, the female must feed her young on milk she has produced.

- The pallid bat of western North America is immune to the stings of scorpions, as well as the seven-inch centipedes upon which it feeds.

- The pelican breathes through its mouth because it has no nostrils.

- To safeguard its food when away, the wolverine marks it with a strong musk so foul smelling that other animals won't touch it.

- The penculine titmouse of Africa builds its home in such a sturdy manner that Masai tribesman use their nests for purses and carrying cases.

- To survive, most birds must eat at least half their own weight in food each day.

—————— **SCIENCE AND NATURE** ——————

- Toads eat only moving prey.

- The penguin is the only bird that can swim, but not fly. It is also the only bird that walks upright.

- Today's oldest form of horse is the Przewalski, or Mongolian Wild Horse. Survivors of this breed were discovered in the Gobi Desert in 1881.

- The pistol shrimp makes a noise so loud that it can shatter glass.

- Travelling at a rate of two to three miles per hour, camels can carry 500 to 1,000 pounds on their backs. They are able to keep up this pace for six or seven hours a day. Camels will refuse to carry loads that are not properly balanced.

- The pitohui bird of Papua New Guinea has enough poison in its feathers and skin to kill mice and frogs. The poison can affect humans, often causing them numbness, burning and sneezing.

- The polar bear is the only bear that has hair on the soles of its feet. This protects the animal's feet from the cold and prevents slipping on the ice.

---------- **SCIENCE AND NATURE** ----------

- Tuna swim at a steady rate of nine miles per hour for an indefinite period of time – and they never stop moving. Estimates indicate that a 15-year-old tuna travels one million miles in its lifetime.

- Tunas will suffocate if they ever stop swimming. They need a continual flow of water across their gills to breathe, even while they rest.

- Turtles survived the upheavals of the last 200 million years, including the great extinction episode that eliminated the dinosaurs. Now, about half of the world's turtle species face possible extinction – due in large part to a growing demand for turtles as a popular dining delicacy and a source of traditional medicines.

- Two rats can become the progenitors of 15,000 rats in less than a year.

- Unlike most fish, electric eels cannot get enough oxygen from water. Approximately every five minutes, they must surface to breathe or they will drown. Unlike most fish, they can swim both backwards and forwards.

- Unlike most other large cats, snow leopards cannot roar.

SCIENCE AND NATURE

- The quahog, a marine clam, can live for up to 200 years, making it the longest living ocean creature in the world. Second place goes to the killer whale at 90 years; third is the blue whale at 80 years; fourth is the sea turtle at 50 years, and fifth is the tiger shark at 40 years.

- The racoon derives its name from the Indian word meaning 'he who scratches with his hands'.

- The acorn woodpecker leaves its food sticking out of the holes it's drilled in oak trees, making it easy for squirrels and jays to help themselves.

- Until he's about 21 years old, the male Indian elephant isn't interested in romancing a female elephant.

- Until they were imported into the country, Australia did not have any members of the cat family, hoofed animals, apes or monkeys.

- Using its web – the skin between its arms – an octopus can carry up to a dozen crabs back to its den.

- Vampire bats adopt orphans and have been known to risk their lives to share food with less fortunate roost-mates.

SCIENCE AND NATURE

- Vampire bats don't suck blood; they drink it. By making small cuts in the skin of a sleeping animal, while their saliva numbs the area, the bat laps up the blood.

- Vampire bats need about two tablespoonfuls of blood each day. The creature is able to extract its dinner in approximately 20 minutes.

- Victorian society rejected the notion that pets were capable of feelings or expressing emotion.

- Walking catfish of Florida can stay out of water for 80 days.

- Wandering albatross devote a full year to raising their babies.

- The best working light-bulb a long time ago was a thread of sheep's wool coated with carbon.

- 107 incorrect medical procedures will be performed by the end of the day today.

- A Boeing 747's wingspan is longer than the Wright brothers' first flight.

SCIENCE AND NATURE

- A bolt of lightning can strike the earth with a force as great as 100 million volts.

- A creep is a metallurgical term for when something that is normally very strong bends because of gravity. This happens to many metals at high temperatures, where they won't melt but they will creep.

- A cubic mile of fog is made up of less than a gallon of water.

- A fierce gust of wind blew 45-year-old Vittorio Luise's car into a river near Naples, Italy, in 1980. He managed to break a window, climb out and swim to shore, where a tree blew over and killed him.

- A fully loaded supertanker travelling at normal speed takes at least 20 minutes to stop.

- A full moon always rises at sunset.

- A full moon is nine times brighter than a half moon.

- A jiffy is an actual unit of time for one-hundredth of a second. Thus the saying, 'I will be there in a jiffy!'

---------- **SCIENCE AND NATURE** ----------

- A large flawless emerald is worth more than a similarly large flawless diamond.

- A lightning bolt generates temperatures five times hotter than those found on the sun's surface.

- A manned rocket can reach the moon in less time than it took a stagecoach to travel the length of England.

- A neutron star has such a powerful gravitational pull that it can spin on its axis in one-thirtieth of a second without tearing itself apart.

- A normal raindrop falls at about seven miles per hour.

- A rainbow can only occur when the sun is 40 degrees or less above the horizon.

- The shell constitutes 12 per cent of an egg's weight.

- A silicon chip a quarter-inch square has the capacity of the original 1949 ENIAC computer, which occupied a city block.

- A standard grave is 7'8 x 3'2 x 6'.

SCIENCE AND NATURE

- A syzygy occurs when three atronomical bodies line up.

- A temperature of 70 million degrees Celsius was generated at Princeton University in 1978. This was during a fusionism experiment and is the highest man-made temperature ever.

- A wind with a speed of 74 miles or more is designated a hurricane.

- About seven million cars are junked each year in the US.

- According to the Texas Department of Transportation, one person is killed annually painting stripes on the state's highways and roads.

- All organic compounds contain carbon.

- All snow crystals are hexagonal.

- All the gold produced in the past 500 years, if melted, could be compressed into a 50-foot cube.

- All totalled, the sunlight that strikes earth at any given moment weighs as much as an ocean liner.

—————— SCIENCE AND NATURE ——————

- An inch of snow falling evenly on one acre of ground is equivalent to about 2,715 gallons of water.

- Any free-moving liquid in outer space will form itself into a sphere because of its surface tension.

- Astronauts in orbit around the earth can see the wakes of ships.

- At any given time, there are 1,800 thunderstorms in progress over the earth's atmosphere.

- At room temperature, the average air molecule travels at the speed of a rifle bullet.

- Back in the mid to late 80s, an IBM-compatible computer wasn't considered a hundred per cent compatible unless it could run Microsoft's Flight Simulator.

- Bacteria, the tiniest free-living cells, are so small that a single drop of liquid contains as many as 50 million of them.

- Bamboo (the world's tallest grass) can grow up to 90cm in a day.

SCIENCE AND NATURE

- Because of the rotation of the earth, an object can be thrown further if it is thrown west.

- By weight, the sun is 70 per cent hydrogen, 28 per cent helium, 1.5 per cent carbon, nitrogen and oxygen, and 0.5 per cent all other elements.

- Clouds fly higher during the day than the night.

- Construction workers hard hats were first invented and used in the building of the Hoover Dam in 1933.

- Diamonds are composed of just one chemical element, carbon.

- Did you know you share a birthday with at least nine other million people in the world?

- DuPont is the world's largest chemical company.

- During the time that the atomic bomb was being hatched by the United States at Alamogordo, New Mexico, applicants for routine jobs like janitors were disqualified if they could read. Illiteracy was a job requirement. The reason: the authorities did not want their rubbish or other papers read.

SCIENCE AND NATURE

- Earth is travelling through space at 660,000 miles per hour.

- February 1865 is the only month in recorded history not to have a full moon.

- Hydrogen is the most common atom in the universe.

- If you attempted to count the stars in a galaxy at a rate of one every second it would take around 3,000 years to count them all.

- If you toss a penny 10,000 times it will not be heads 5,000 times but more like 4,950. The head picture weighs more, so it ends up on the bottom.

- If you yelled for eight years, seven months and six days, you would have produced enough sound energy to heat one cup of coffee.

- In 1949, forecasting the relentless march of science, *Popular Mechanics* said computers in the future may weigh no more than five tons.

- Iron nails cannot be used in oak because the acid in the wood corrodes them.

SCIENCE AND NATURE

- In 1961, MIT student Steve Russell, created SPACEWARS, the first interactive computer game, on a Digital PDP-1 (Programmed Data Processor-1) mainframe computer. Limited by the computer technology of the time, ASCII text characters were the 'graphics' and people could only play the game on a device that took up the floorspace of a small house.

- It takes one 15- 20-year-old tree to produce 700 paper grocery bags.

- It takes the insect-eating Venus Flytrap plant only half a second to shut its trap on its prey.

- Japan's currency is the most difficult to counterfeit.

- Lab tests can detect traces of alcohol in urine six to 12 hours after a person has stopped drinking.

- Life on earth probably developed in an oxygen-free atmosphere. Even today there are microorganisms that can live only in the absence of oxygen.

- Mercury is the only metal that is liquid at room temperature.

SCIENCE AND NATURE

- Methane gas can often be seen bubbling up from the bottom of ponds. It is produced by the decomposition of dead plants and animals in the mud.

- Moisture, not air, causes superglue to dry.

- Robots in Japan pay union dues.

- The shortest intercontinental commercial flight in the world is from Gibraltar (Europe) to Tangier (Africa.) Distance: 34 miles; flight time: 20 minutes.

- Stainless steel was discovered by accident in 1913.

- Stars come in different colours; hot stars give off blue light and the cooler stars give off red light.

- The Apollo 11 had only 20 seconds of fuel left when it landed.

- The ashes of the metal magnesium are heavier than magnesium itself.

- The bark of a redwood tree is fireproof. Fires that occur in a redwood forest take place inside the trees.

——————— SCIENCE AND NATURE ———————

- The Boeing 737 jet is nicknamed 'Fat Albert.'

- The Boeing 747 has been in commercial service since 1970.

- The colour black is produced by the complete absorption of light rays.

- The company Kodak is the largest user of silver.

- The densest substance on earth is the metal 'osmium.'

- The first American submarine was built around 1776.

- The first atomic bomb exploded at Trinity Site, New Mexico.

- The first computer ever made was called ENIAC.

- The leaves of the Victorian water lily are sometimes over six feet in diameter.

- The 111th element is known as unnilenilenium

- The process of splitting atoms is called fission.

SCIENCE AND NATURE

- The Saguaro Cactus, found in the Southwestern United States, doesn't grow branches until it is 75 years old.

- The shockwave from a nitroglycerine explosion travels at 17,000 miles per hour.

- The Sitka spruce is Britain's most commonly planted tree.

- The smallest unit of time is the yoctosecond.

- The speed of sound must be exceeded to produce a sonic boom.

- The strength of early lasers was measured in Gillettes, the number of blue razor blades a given beam could puncture.

- The tail section of an airplane gives the bumpiest ride.

- The tip of a bullwhip moves so fast that it breaks the sound barrier; the crack of the whip is actually a tiny sonic boom.

- The total quantity of energy in the universe is constant.

———— SCIENCE AND NATURE ————

- The Venus flytrap can eat a whole cheeseburger.

- There are five tillion trillion atoms in one pound of iron.

- Twenty years make up a vicennial period.

- When CBS broadcast the first television show in colour, no one other than CBS owned a colour television set.

- When glass breaks, the cracks move at speeds up to 3,000 miles per hour.

- You are most likely to lose your hearing than any of the other senses if you are hit by lightning.

5

LITERATURE
AND ART

LITERATURE AND ART

- In the book *Gone With the Wind*, Melanie's pregnancy lasts 21 months – based on the actual battles mentioned.

- Author Ian Fleming gave the name James Bond to his spy hero after seeing it on the cover of a book of West Indian birds, by ornithologist James Bond.

- When asked to name his favourite among all his paintings Pablo Picasso replied 'the next one'.

- Mick Jagger turned down a £3.5 million advance offer on his memoirs from a publisher because, he said, he 'couldn't remember' enough significant details from his own life.

- The part of Hamlet, by William Shakespeare, is the longest of the playwright's speaking parts with 1,530 lines. The second longest part is that of Richard III with 1,164 lines.

- Agatha Christie claimed she did most of the plotting for her detective stories while sitting in a bath tub eating apples.

LITERATURE AND ART

- Disney cleaned up the story of *Snow White and the Seven Dwarfs* for his feature cartoon. In the original Grimm Brothers fairytale the Queen was condemned to dance in red-hot iron shoes until she died. Disney had her falling of a precipice to her death.

- It was a combination of the two words 'will comply' that produced the radio-code response 'wilco'.

- Gambrinous is a word meaning being full of beer.

- Author Lewis Carroll combined the words 'chuckle' and 'snort' to come up with the word 'chortle' in *Through the Looking Glass*.

- Transurphobia is the fear of haircuts.

- Dylan Thomas once unkindly pointed out that, except for one misplaced letter, T S Eliot's name spelled backwards is 'Toilets'.

- The first names of Dr Jekyll and Mr Hyde were Henry and Edward.

- Dr Frankenstein's first name was Victor.

--------- **LITERATURE AND ART** ---------

- 'Able was I ere I saw Elba' is a palindrome written by Napoleon.

- One edition of the current *Sunday New York Times* has more information in it than a typical adult was exposed to in an entire lifetime a hundred years ago.

- The slow-witted character named Moron in Molière's play *La Princesse d'Elide* created a new word in the dictionary.

- The International Association of Women Helicopter Pilots is known as the Whirly Girls.

- Ezra Pound, William Joyce and P G Wodehouse all made broadcasts for the enemy during World War II.

- The pasta vermicelli means 'little worms'.

- Charles Dickens penned in Puny Pete, Little Larry and Small Sam before settling on Tiny Tim for his crippled child in *A Christmas Carol*.

- Oscar Wilde once remarked that, 'America was often discovered before Columbus, but it was always hushed up.'

LITERATURE AND ART

- The term 'maverick' came from Texas rancher Sam Maverick, who refused to brand his calves.

- The line 'Three quarks for Muster Mark!' in James Joyce's *Ulysses* provided the name for the subatomic particles now known as 'quarks', named by physicist Murray Gell-Mann.

- The 'y' in old words like 'ye' is better pronounced with a 'th' sound and not a 'y' sound. In Latin the 'th' sound did not exist and the Romans occupying England used the rune 'thorne' to represent the 'th' sounds. When the printing presses were invented the character from the Roman alphabet which most closely resembled the 'thorne' was the lower case 'y'.

- The phrase 'United we stand, divided we fall' was first used in the Aesop fable *The Four Oxen and the Lion*, written nearly 600 years before Christ.

- Charles Dickens took just six weeks to write *A Christmas Carol*.

- The highest scoring three-letter word in Scrabble is Zax, which is a tool for cutting and trimming roof slates.

────── LITERATURE AND ART ──────

- The letters of the word 'SHAZAM', which was shouted to conjure up comic-book hero Captain Marvel, stood for Solomon's Wisdom, Hercules's Strength, Atlas's Stamina, Zeus's Power, Achilles's Courage and Mercury's Speed.

- The first name of Jeeves, the fictional butler created by P G Woodhouse in 1915, remained a mystery for many years (even to his employer). It was later revealed in his 1971 novel *Much Obliged Jeeves*. His name was Reginald.

- A trilemma is a dilemma with a third alternative.

- The most commonly used word in English conversation is 'I'.

- There are twenty different kinds of kisses described in the erotic Indian text the *Kama Sutra*.

- The writer Edgar Allen Poe and singer Jerry Lee Lewis both married their thirteen-year-old cousins.

- Popeye the sailorman's home port was called Sweetwater.

LITERATURE AND ART

- The first time Goofy appeared in a Mickey Mouse cartoon he was known as Dippy Dawg. He was renamed in the 1930s when he began to star regularly with Mickey.

- In the US strip cartoon *Blondie* Dagwood once remarked: 'The trouble with the rat race is that there is never a finish line.'

- The Aboriginal word 'koala' means 'no drink'. The Australian creature gets all its liquid and food from eucalyptus leaves.

- The only word in the English language that both begins and ends with the letters 'und' is 'underground'.

- Dr Watson's bullet wound moved according to different Sherlock Holmes stories. In *A Study in Scarlet* it was in his shoulder but in *The Sign of Four* it was in his leg.

- Edgar Allen Poe was expelled from West Point Military Academy for turning out on a public parade wearing only his white belt and gloves.

─────── LITERATURE AND ART ───────

- One seven-letter word that contains ten other words without any of the letters being rearranged is 'therein'. It includes 'the', 'there', 'he', 'in', 'rein', 'her', 'here', 'ere', 'therein' and 'herein'.

- During World War I Agatha Christie worked in a hospital dispensary and it is there she acquired her extensive knowledge of poisons.

- The first complete bible printed in the United States was in the language of the Algonquian Indians. It was translated and published in 1663 by the Reverend John Eliot.

- In Africa the house of the wicked witch in *Hansel and Gretel* is not made of gingerbread but of salt – which is highly prized by children.

- 'Strengths' is the longest word in the English language with just one vowel.

- During World War II there were two types of dirigibles – the A-rigid and the B-limp. The second became the common-usage name for a dirigible – blimp.

LITERATURE AND ART

- The Nepalese word for the Abominable Snowman is *Metohkangmi*, which means 'the indescribably filthy man of the snow'.

- The first person who referred to a coward as a chicken was William Shakespeare.

- Virginia Woolf wrote all her books standing up.

- The original meaning of the word 'clue' was a ball of thread or yarn. Like its modern namesake, it often took some time to unravel.

- Medieval ecclesiastical calendars had the important saints and feast days highlighted in red ink. These memorable days became known as 'red-letter days'.

- In olden days the top crust of a loaf of bread would always be presented to the king, or highest-ranking person, at the table. Hence the expression 'upper crust' for high-ranking people.

- An American billion is 1,000 million – a British billion is 1,000,000 million.

---------- **LITERATURE AND ART** ----------

- The full medical description of a black eye is 'bilateral perorbital haematoma'.

- 'Queuetopia' was a word invented by Winston Churchill to describe communist countries where people had to line up to buy anything.

- A nineteenth-century advertisement for a McCoy sewing machine introduced the phrase 'The real McCoy' into the English language.

- The word 'spam' is an acronym formed from SPiced hAM.

- A duffle bag is so called because the thick wool originally used to make the bags came from the Belgium town of Duffle.

- Arthur Conan Doyle was awarded a knighthood for his defence of the British concentration camps during the Boer Wars and not because of his Sherlock Holmes stories.

- The difference between a nook and a cranny is that the nook is a corner and the cranny is a crack.

——————— LITERATURE AND ART ———————

- The American State Department refers to elevators as 'vertical transportation units'.

- Race car is a palindrome.

- Shakespeare's daughters were called Susanna and Judith.

- It was US critic, author and poet Dorothy Parker who wrote 'Men don't make passes at girls who wear glasses.'

- The word 'robot' comes from the Czechoslovakian word '*robotovat*', which means to work very hard. It was created by Karel Capek.

- John Steinbeck worked as a hod carrier, conveying concrete along scaffolding during the construction of New York's Madison Square Garden in the 1930s.

- Playwright Tom Stoppard's native language is Czechoslovakian. His Czech mother married an English army officer named Stoppard.

- According to Ernest Hemingway four achievements are necessary to become a real man. You should plant a tree, fight a bull, write a book and have a son.

————— LITERATURE AND ART —————

- The term 'strike' originated in 1768 when British sailors refused to work and showed this by striking, or lowering, the sails on their ships.

- The letters HIOX in the Latin alphabet are the only ones that look the same if you turn them upside down or see them from behind.

- The English word 'indivisibility' has only one vowel that occurs six times.

- 'Facetiously' and 'abstemiously' are the only two words in the English language that contain all the vowels, including 'y', in alphabetical order.

- The English syllable 'ough' can be pronounced nine different ways. One sentence that contains them all is: 'A rough-coated, dough-faced thoughtful ploughman strode through the streets of Scarborough and after falling into his slough he coughed and hiccoughed.'

- Left-handed people cannot write Mandarin Chinese.

- The contraction of the Middle Ages phrase 'God be with ye' produced the modern word 'goodbye'.

LITERATURE AND ART

- *Bambi* was originally published in 1929 in German.

- During his entire lifetime, Herman Melville's timeless classic of the sea *Moby Dick*, only sold 50 copies.

- General Lew Wallace's bestseller *Ben Hur* was the first work of fiction to be blessed by a pope.

- *Guinness Book of Records* holds the record for being the book most often stolen from public libraries.

- In 1898 (14 years prior to the *Titanic* tragedy), Morgan Robertson wrote a novel called *Futility*. This fictitious novel was about the largest ship ever built hitting an iceberg in the Atlantic ocean on a cold April night.

- Mary Shelley wrote *Frankenstein* at the age of 19.

- The all time bestselling electronic book is Stephen King's *Riding The Bullet*.

- The Bible is the number one shoplifted book in America.

- The book of Esther in the Bible is the only book which does not mention the name of God.

--------- **LITERATURE AND ART** ---------

- The only person to decline a Pulitzer Prize for Fiction was Sinclair Lewis for his book *Arrowsmith*.

- *Tom Sawyer* was the first novel written on a typewriter.

- A castrated rooster is called a capon.

- A deltiologist collects postcards.

- A fingerprint is also known as a dactylogram.

- A funambulist is a tightrope walker.

- A gynaephobic man fears women.

- A phrenologist feels and interprets skull features.

- A sultan's wife is called a sultana.

- An anthropophagist eats people.

- Killing a king is called regicide.

- Narcissism is the psychiatric term for self-love.

LITERATURE AND ART

- Of all the words in the English language, the word 'set' has the most definitions.

- Paedophobia is a fear of children.

- Rhythm and syzygy are the longest English words without vowels.

- Scuba stands for 'Self-contained underwater breathing apparatus'.

- Sheriff came from Shire Reeve. During early years of feudal rule in England, each shire had a reeve who was the law for that shire. When the term was taken to the United States it was shortened to sheriff.

- Skepticisms is the longest typed word that alternates hands.

- Spat-out food is called chanking.

- Taphephobia is the fear of being buried alive.

- The letter J does not appear anywhere on the periodic table of elements.

—————— LITERATURE AND ART ——————

- The letter W is the only letter in the alphabet that doesn't have one syllable, it has three.

- The longest one-syllable word in the English language is screeched.

- The longest word in the English language is 1909 letters long and it refers to a distinct part of DNA.

- The most used letter in the English alphabet is E, and Q is the least used.

- The oldest word in the English language is town.

- The only 15-letter word that can be spelled without repeating a letter is uncopyrightable.

- The only contemporary words that end with gry are angry and hungry.

- The phrase 'rule of thumb' is derived from an old English law stating that you cannot beat your wife with anything wider than your thumb.

LITERATURE AND ART

- The phrase sleep tight originated when mattresses were set upon ropes woven through the bed frame. To remedy sagging ropes, one would use a bed key to tighten the rope.

- The U in U-boats stands for 'under water'.

- The word constipation comes from a Latin word that means 'to crowd together'.

- The word racecar and kayak are palindromes: the same whether they are read left to right or right to left.

- The word samba means to rub navels together.

- The words assassination and bump were invented by Shakespeare.

- There are only four words in the English language which end in -dous: tremendous, horrendous, stupendous and hazardous.

- There are only three world capitals that begin with the letter O in English: Ottawa, Canada; Oslo, Norway; and Ouagadougou, Burkina Faso.

LITERATURE AND ART

- There are six words in the English language with the letter combination uu. Muumuu, vacuum, continuum, duumvirate, duumvir and residuum.

- There are 10 body parts that are only three letters long: eye, ear, leg, arm, jaw, gum, toe, lip, hip and rib.

- There was no punctuation until the 15th century.

- Tonsurphobia is the fear of haircuts.

- When two words are combined to form a single word (e.g. motor + hotel = motel, breakfast + lunch = brunch) the new word is called a portmanteau.

- When your sink is full, the little hole that lets the water drain, instead of flowing over the side, is called a porcelator.

- Women who wink at men are known as 'nictitating' women.

- You would have to count to one thousand to use the letter A in the English language to spell a whole number.

LITERATURE AND ART

- A baby eel is called an elver; a baby oyster is called a spat.

- A Flemish artist is responsible for the world's smallest painting in history. It is a picture of a miller and his mill, and it was painted on to a grain of corn.

- A group of crows is called a murder.

- A group of officers is called a mess.

- A lump of pure gold the size of a matchbox car can be flattened into a sheet the size of a tennis court.

- All Hebrew originating names that end with the letters 'el' have something to do with God.

- Arachibutyrophobia is the fear of peanut butter sticking to the roof of your mouth.

- Arnold Schonberg suffered from triskaidecphobia, the fear of the number 13. He died 13 minutes from midnight on Friday the 13th.

- Bookkeeper is the only word in the English language with three consecutive double letters.

LITERATURE AND ART

- Chevrolet tried marketing a Chevrolet Nova in Spanish – speaking countries – it didn't sell well because NO VA means 'doesn't go' in Spanish.

- Clinophobia is the fear of beds.

- Corduroy comes from the French, *cord du roi* or 'cloth of the king'.

- Dibble means to drink like a duck.

- During his entire life, Vincent Van Gogh sold only one painting, *Red Vineyard at Arles*.

- Dutch painter Vincent Van Gogh cut off his left ear. His *Self-portrait with the Bandaged Ear* shows the right one bandaged because he painted the mirror image.

- Ernest Vincent Wright wrote the 50,000 – word novel *Gatsby* without any word containing 'e'.

- Facetious and abstemious contain all the vowels in the correct order, as does arsenious, meaning containing arsenic.

———— LITERATURE AND ART ————

- Ghosts appear in four Shakespearian plays; *Julius Caesar*, *Richard III*, *Hamlet* and *Macbeth*.

- Great Britain was the first county to issue postage stamps. Hence, the postage stamps of Britain are the only stamps in the world not to bear the name of the country of origin. However, every stamp carries a relief image or a silhouette of the monarch's head instead.

- Groaking is to watch people eating in the hope that they will offer you some.

- Hara kiri is an impolite way of saying the Japanese word *seppuku* which means, literally, belly splitting.

- Hydroxydesoxycorticosterone and hydroxydeoxycorticosterones are the largest anagrams.

- 'I am'. is the shortest complete sentence in the English language.

- If each count were one second long, it would take about 12 days to count to a million and 32 years to count to a billion.

LITERATURE AND ART

- If you look carefully at the picture of the *Mona Lisa*, you will notice a bridge in the background.

- In England, in the 1880s pants was considered a dirty word.

- In English, four is the only digit that has the same number of letters as its value.

- In Ethiopia, both males and females of the Surma tribes shave their heads as a mark of beauty.

- In Italy, a campaign for Schweppes Tonic Water translated the name into Schweppes Toilet Water.

- In most advertisements, including newspapers, the time displayed on a watch is 10:10.

- In Papua New Guinea, there are villages within five miles of each other which speak different languages.

- In the 40s, the Bich pen was changed to Bic for fear that Americans would pronounce it 'Bitch'.

- Influenza got its name from the fact that people believed the disease was because of the evil 'influence' of stars.

——————— LITERATURE AND ART ———————

- It is believed that Shakespeare was 46 around the time that the King James Version of the Bible was written. In Psalms 46, the 46th word from the first word is shake and the 46th word from the last word is spear.

- It is possible to drown and not die. Technically the term 'drowning' refers to the process of taking water into the lungs, not to death caused by that process.

- Jet lag was once called boat lag, before there were jets.

- Karaoke means empty orchestra in Japanese.

- Lead poisoning is known as plumbism.

- Libra, the scales, is the only inanimate symbol in the zodiac.

- Maine is the only state whose name is just one syllable.

- Naked means to be unprotected; nude means unclothed.

- Native speakers of Japanese learn Spanish more easily than English. Native speakers of English learn Spanish more easily than Japanese.

LITERATURE AND ART

- Nine is considered the luckiest number worldwide.

- No word in the English language rhymes with month, orange, silver or purple.

- Nova Scotia is Latin for New Scotland.

- 19 November is 'Have a Bad Day day'.

- Nycrophobia is the fear of darkness.

- Papaphobia is the fear of popes.

- People didn't always say hello when they answered the phone. When the first regular phone service was established in 1878, people said Ahoy.

- Polish is the only word in the English language that when capitalized is changed from a noun or a verb to a nationality.

- Put a sock in it: be quiet, shut-up, make less noise; a slang expression. In the late 19th century and earlier years of the 20th century, when gramophones or phonographs amplified the sound through large horns, woollen socks were often stuffed in them to cut down the noise.

LITERATURE AND ART

- Quisling is the only word in the English language to start with 'quis'.

- Scatologists are experts who study poop (aka crap, dung, dookie, dumps, faeces, excrement, etc.)

- Sekkusu is sex in Japanese.

- 'Smithee' is a pseudonym that filmmakers use when they don't want their names to appear in the credits.

- Son of a gun: this familiar designation implying contempt but now used with jocular familiarity derives from the days when women were allowed to live in naval ships. The son of the gun was one born in the ship often near the midship gun, behind canvas screen. If the paternity was uncertain, the child was entered in the log as 'son of a gun'.

- Spain literally means 'the land of rabbits'.

- Stewardesses is the longest word that is typed with only the left hand.

LITERATURE AND ART

- Strange- but -real college courses offered advanced cereal science, amusement park administration, clay wheel throwing, fatherhood and soil judging.

- The 'a.m.' in 5:00 a.m. stands for ante meridiem.

- The abbreviation 'e.g.' stands for 'Exempli gratia', or 'For example.'

- The abbreviation for one pound, lb, comes from the astrological sign Libra meaning balance.

- The Bible has been translated into Klingon.

- The correct response to the Irish greeting 'Top of the morning to you', is 'And the rest of the day to yourself'.

- The earliest document in Latin in a woman's handwriting (it is from the first century AD) is an invitation to a birthday party.

- The Eskimo language has over 20 words to describe different kinds of snow.

———————— **LITERATURE AND ART** ————————

- The expletive 'Holy Toledo' refers to Toledo, Spain, which became an outstanding Christian cultural centre in 1085.

- The expression 'What in tarnation' comes from the original meaning 'What in eternal damnation'.

- The French term 'bourrage de crane' for wartime propaganda means brain stuffing.

- The Kentucky Fried Chicken slogan 'finger-lickin' good' came out as 'eat your fingers off' in Chinese.

- The leading female singer in an opera is called the prima donna.

- The letters KGB stand for Komitet Gosudarstvennoy Bezopasnos.

- The longest place name still in use is: Taumatawhakatangihangaoauauotameteaturipukakapikim aungahoronukupokaiw-henuakitanatahu – a New Zealand hill.

—————— LITERATURE AND ART ——————

- The longest place name in Great Britain is that of a Welsh village: Gorsafawddachaidraigddanheddogleddollonpenrhynareur draethceredigion.

- The magic word 'Abracadabra' was originally intended for the specific purpose of curing hay fever.

- The monastic hours are matins, lauds, prime, tierce, sext, nones, vespers and compline.

- The most reverse charge calls are made on Father's Day.

- The most common name for a goldfish is 'Jaws'.

- The most common name in the world is Mohammed.

- The most difficult tongue-twister is 'The sixth sick Sheik's sixth sheep's sick'.

- The name fez is Turkish for hat.

- The national anthem of Greece has 158 verses.

—————— LITERATURE AND ART ——————

- The national anthem of the Netherlands, 'Het Wilhelmus', is an acrostichon. The first letters of each of the 15 verses represent the name Willem Van Nassov.

- The Netherlands and the United States both have anthems that do not mention their country's name.

- The next-to-last event is the penultimate, and the second-to-last is the antepenultimate.

- The nursery rhyme 'Ring A Roses' is a rhyme about the plague. Infected people with the plague would get red circular sores (ring of roses); these sores would smell very badly so common folk would put flowers on their bodies somewhere inconspicuously, so that it would cover the smell of the sores (pocket full of posies).

- *The Practitioner*, a British medical journal, has determined that bird-watching may be hazardous to your health. The magazine, in fact, has officially designated bird-watching a hazardous hobby, after documenting the death of a weekend bird-watcher who became so immersed in his subject that he grew oblivious to his surroundings and consequently was eaten by a crocodile.

LITERATURE AND ART

- The Sanskrit word for 'war' means 'desire for more cows.'

- The slang word crap comes from T. Crapper, the man who invented the modern toilet.

- The term 'cop' came from Constable on Patrol. It is from England.

- The term 'devil's advocate' comes from the Roman Catholic church. When deciding if someone should be sainted, a devil's advocate is always appointed to give an alternative view.

- The term 'mayday' used for signalling for help (after SOS) comes from the French *M'aidez*, which, pronounced Mayday and means help me.

- The term 'the Boogey man will get you' comes from the Boogy people who still inhabit an area of Indonesia. These people still act as pirates today and attack ships that pass.

- The three best-known western names in China: Jesus Christ, Richard Nixon and Elvis Presley.

—————— LITERATURE AND ART ——————

● The word 'kangaroo' means 'I don't know' in the language of Australian Aborigines. When Captain Cook approached natives of the Endeavor River tribe to ask what the strange animal was, he got 'kangaroo' for an answer.

● The word 'Karate' means empty hand.

● The word byte is a contraction of by eight.

● There are about 5,000 different languages spoken on earth.

● There are only 12 letters in the Hawaiian alphabet.

● X-ray technology has shown there are three different versions of the *Mona Lisa* under the visible one.

● Zorro means fox in Spanish.

6

BUSINESS WORLD

BUSINESS WORLD

- A single share of Coca-Cola stock, purchased in 1919, when the company went public, would have been worth $92,500 in 1997.

- It takes about 63,000 trees to make the newsprint for the average Sunday edition of *The New York Times*.

- Nestlé is the largest company in Switzerland, yet more than 98 per cent of its revenue comes from outside the country.

- Organized crime is estimated to account for 10% of the United States' national income.

- The three most valuable brand names on earth are Marlboro, Coca-Cola, and Budweiser, in that order.

- The largest employer in the world is the Indian railway system, employing over a million people.

- The most dangerous job in the United States is that of sanitation worker. Fire fighters and police officers are a close second and third, followed by leather tanners in fourth.

BUSINESS WORLD

- The sale of vodka makes up 10 per cent of Russian Government income.

- The slogan on New Hampshire licence plates is 'Live Free or Die'. These licence plates are manufactured by prisoners in the state prison in Concord.

- Workers at Matsushita Electric Company in Japan beat dummies of their foremen with bamboo sticks to let off steam. The company has enjoyed 30 per cent growth for 25 consecutive years.

7

USELESS
THINGS PEOPLE
SAY

——— USELESS THINGS PEOPLE SAY ———

● 'I'm one of those stupid bums who never went to university, and it hasn't done me any harm.'

Prince Philip

● 'I'm one of those stupid bums who went to university. Well, I think it's helped me.'

Prince Charles

● 'Children today are tyrants. They contradict their parents, gobble their food and tyrannise their teachers. I despair for the future.'

Socrates, 400 BC

● 'Outside consultants sought for test of gas chamber.'

Arizona Republic ad

● 'Those who survived the San Francisco earthquake said: "Thank God I'm still alive." But, of course, those who died, their lives will never be the same again.'

US Senator Barbara Boxer

● 'Most lies about blondes are false.'

Cincinnati Times-Star

● 'Maybe this world is another planet's Hell.'

Aldous Huxley

──── USELESS THINGS PEOPLE SAY ────

● 'Cod are not very good swimmers so are easily overtaken by trawlers and nets.'
Ministry explanation of diminishing North Sea cod

● 'A lie gets halfway around the world before the truth has a chance to get its pants on.'
Sir Winston Churchill

● 'Most cars on our roads have only one occupant, usually the driver.'
Carol Malia, BBC TV presenter

● 'The Holocaust was an obscene period in our nation's history. I mean in this century's history. But we all lived in this century. I didn't live in this century.'
US Vice-President Dan Quayle

● 'I've just learned about his illness. Let's hope it's nothing trivial.'
US reporter/writer Irvin S Cobb

● Movie star Tallulah Bankhead once described herself as 'Pure as the driven slush'.

● 'The only way to get rid of a temptation is to yield to it.'
Oscar Wilde

——— USELESS THINGS PEOPLE SAY ———

● 'We are not ready for an unforeseen event that may or may not occur.'

> *US Vice-President Dan Quayle*

● 'In America, anybody can be president. That's one of the risks you take.'

> *US politican and diplomat Adlai Stevenson*

● 'We don't like their sound. Groups of guitars are on the way out.'

> *Decca Records, speaking about the Beatles*

● 'A billion here, a billion there, sooner or later it adds up to real money.'

> *Congressman Everett Dirksen*

● 'You can get more with a kind word and a gun than you can with a kind word alone.'

> *Al Capone*

● 'A man in love is incomplete until he is married. Then he is finished.'

> *Zsa Zsa Gabor*

● 'I worship the quicksand he walks in.'

> *US political humourist Art Buchwald*

——— USELESS THINGS PEOPLE SAY ———

- 'If it weren't for electricity we'd all be watching television by candlelight.'

  US actor/comedian George Gobel

- 'A pessimist sees the difficulty in every opportunity; an optimist sees the opportunity in every difficulty.'

  Sir Winston Churchill

- 'Does the album have any songs you like that aren't on it?'

  Music reviewer Harry News

- 'Fiction writing is great. You can make up almost anything.'

  Ivana Trump – after her first novel was published

- 'We're going to move left and right at the same time.'

  California governor Jerry Brown

- 'The word genius isn't applicable in football. A genius is a guy like Norman Einstein.'

  Sports analyst Joe Theisman

- 'We talked five times. He called me twice and I called him twice.'

  California Angels coach

──── USELESS THINGS PEOPLE SAY ────

- 'If I had as many love affairs as you have given me credit
  for, I would now be speaking to you from a jar in the
  Harvard Medical School.'

  Frank Sinatra, speaking to reporters

- 'If you take out the killings, Washington actually has a
  very low crime rate.'

  The Mayor of Washington

- 'That's just the tip of the ice cube.'

  Former Tory MP Neil Hamilton, speaking on BBC2

- 'Whether you think that you can, or that you can't, you
  are usually right.'

  Henry Ford

- 'I'd rather be dead than singing "Satisfaction"
  when I'm 45.'

  Mick Jagger

- 'We are not without accomplishment. We have managed
  to distribute poverty equally.'

  Vietnam's Foreign Minister

- 'Good-looking people turn me off, myself included.'

  Patrick Swayze

—————— **USELESS THINGS PEOPLE SAY** ——————

● 'Danger. Slow men at work.'

Brunei road sign

● 'Never interrupt your enemy when he is making a mistake.'

Napoleon Bonaparte

● 'Ladies are requested not to have children at the bar.'

Norwegian bar notice

● 'I may be dumb but I'm not stupid.'

US Football announcer Terry Bradshaw

● 'The longer I live the more I see that I am never wrong about anything, and that all the pains that I have so humbly taken to verify my notions have only wasted my time.'

George Bernard Shaw

● 'And as Mansell comes into the pits, he's quite literally sweating his eyeballs out.'

British TV commentator

● 'My Lord, we find the man who stole the mare not guilty.'

Welsh jury foreman

———— USELESS THINGS PEOPLE SAY ————

- 'To love oneself is the beginning of a lifelong romance.'
  Oscar Wilde

- 'I patterned my look after Cinderella, Mother Goose and the local hooker.'
  Dolly Parton, speaking in an interview

- The *two types of men* Mae West said she preferred 'Domestic and foreign.'

- 'It was not my kind of people. There wasn't a producer, a press agent, a director or an actor.'
  Zsa Zsa Gabor, about her trial jury

- 'Hi, I'm Dean White. Dick of the college.'
  Duke University dean Richard White

- 'I invented the internet.'
  US Vice-President Al Gore

- 'Most hotels are already booked solid by people, plus 5,000 journalists.'
  Bangkok Post

- 'Life is very important to Americans.'
  US Senator Bob Dole

——— USELESS THINGS PEOPLE SAY ———

● 'My favourite programme is *Mrs Dale's Diary*. I try never to miss it because it is the only way of knowing what goes on in a middle-class family.'

The Queen Mother

● 'If you walk backwards, you'll find out that you can go forwards and people won't know if you're coming or going.'

Baseball manager Casey Stengel

● 'The team has come along slow but fast.'

Baseball manager Casey Stengel

● 'People that are really very weird can get into sensitive positions and have a tremendous impact on history.'

US Vice-President Dan Quayle

● 'And now the sequence of events in no particular order.'

CBS news anchorman Dan Rather

● 'Weather forecast: Precipitation in the morning, rain in the afternoon.'

Detroit Daily News

● 'Make everything as simple as possible, but not simpler.'

Albert Einstein

——— USELESS THINGS PEOPLE SAY ———

● 'You'd better learn secretarial work – or else get married.'
> *Model agent Emmeline Strively, speaking to*
> *Marilyn Monroe in 1944*

● 'I've read about foreign policy and studied – I know the number of continents.'
> *US presidential candidate George Wallace*

● 'It is white.'
> *President George W Bush, describing the White House*

● 'The true measure of a man is how he treats someone who can do him absolutely no good.'
> *Samuel Johnson*

● 'Teeth extracted by the latest Methodists.'
> *Hong Kong dental ad*

● 'I don't like this word "bomb". It is not a bomb but a device that is exploding.'
> *French Ambassador Jacques Leblanc,*
> *speaking on nuclear weapons*

● 'I find that the harder I work, the more luck I seem to have.'
> *US President Thomas Jefferson*

———— USELESS THINGS PEOPLE SAY ————

● 'When choosing between two evils, I always like to try the one I've never tried before.'

Mae West

● 'In a sense it's a one-man show. Except there are two men involved.'

John Motson, BBC sports commentator

● 'Only two things are infinite, the universe and human stupidity, and I'm not sure about the former.'

Albert Einstein

● 'I don't diet. I just don't eat as much as I'd like to.'

Supermodel Linda Evangelista

● 'I used to be Snow White, but I drifted.'

Mae West

● 'Now there's a broad with her future behind her.'

Fellow performer Constance Bennett, describing the young Marilyn Monroe

● 'Politics gives guys so much power that they tend to behave badly around women. And I hope I never get into that.'

US President Bill Clinton

──── USELESS THINGS PEOPLE SAY ────

● 'I don't know anything about music. In my line you don't have to.'

Elvis Presley

● 'Pitching is 80% of the game. The other half is hitting and fielding.'

Baseball player Mickey Rivers

● 'I think you can't repeat the first time of something.'

Singer Natalie Imbruglia

● 'Glory is fleeting, but obscurity is forever.'

Napoleon Bonaparte

● 'Sometimes they write what I say and not what I mean.'

Baseball player Pedro Guerrero – about the press

● When John Houston cast his daughter, Anjelica, in a leading role in *A Walk with Love and Death* – her film debut – she was panned by the critics. One wrote: 'She has the face of an exhausted gnu, the voice of an unstrung tennis racket and a figure of no describable shape.'

● 'Permitted vehicles not allowed.'

Road sign on US Highway 27

———— USELESS THINGS PEOPLE SAY ————

● 'Wonderful bargains for men with 16 and 17 necks.'

Clothing store sign

● 'If history repeats itself I should think we can expect the same thing again.'

Terry Venables

● 'We didn't lose. We weren't beaten. We just came in second.'

US commentator at 1996 Olympics

● 'I've never had major knee surgery on any other part of my body.'

Basketball player Winston Bennet

● 'To make women learned and foxes tame has the same defect – to make them more cunning.'

King James I

● 'How would you like to make a thousand speeches and never once be allowed to say what you think yourself?'

King Edward VIII to Churchill

● 'If you can count your money, you don't have a billion dollars.'

J Paul Getty

——— USELESS THINGS PEOPLE SAY ———

- 'I really didn't say everything I said.'
  'Always go to other people's funerals, otherwise they won't go to yours.'
  'It's like déjà vu all over again.'
  'Predictions are difficult, especially about the future.'
  'A nickel ain't worth a dime any more.'

  Baseball player Yogi Berra

- 'You look after your Empire and I will look after my life.'

  Princess Margaret – after being reproached by the Queen

- 'Whenever I watch TV and I see those poor starving kids all over the world, I can't help but cry. I mean I would love to be skinny like that, but not with all those flies and death and stuff.'

  Singer Mariah Carey

- 'If women didn't exist, all the money in the world would have no meaning.'

  Aristotle Onassis

- 'The doctors X-rayed my head and found nothing.'

  Baseball player Dizzy Dean

- 'The covers of this book are too far apart.'

  US newspaper columnist and novelist Ambrose Bierce

———— **USELESS THINGS PEOPLE SAY** ————

● 'I shall go back to bed. I have never slept with a Queen before.'

> *King William IV – on acceding to the throne*

● 'Knowledge speaks, but wisdom listens.'

> *Jimi Hendrix*

● 'Sure there have been injuries and deaths in boxing, but none of them serious.'

> *Boxer Alan Minter*

● 'Whatever is begun in anger ends in shame.'

> *US statesman and scientist Benjamin Franklin*

● 'I wish men had boobs because I like the feel of them. It's so funny, when I record I sing with a hand over each of them. Maybe it's a comfort thing.'

> *Singer Emma Bunton (Baby Spice)*

● 'The internet is a great way to get on the net.'

> *US presidential candidate Bob Dole*

● 'Hawaii is a unique state. It is a state that is by itself. It is different from the other 49 states. Well, all states are different, but it's got a particularly unique situation.'

> *US Vice-President Dan Quayle*

——— USELESS THINGS PEOPLE SAY ———

- 'I am often asked whether it is through some genetic trait that I stand with my hands behind my back like my father. The answer is that we both have the same tailor. He makes our sleeves so tight that we can't get our hands in front.'

  Prince Charles

- 'You got to be careful if you don't know where you're going, because you might not get there.'

  Baseball player Yogi Berra

- 'My sister's expecting a baby, and I don't know if I'm going to be an uncle or an aunt.'

  Basketball player Chuck Nevitt

- 'Reality is merely an illusion, albeit a very persistent one.'

  Albert Einstein

- 'If you give a person a fish, they'll fish for a day. But if you train a person to fish, they'll fish for a lifetime.'

  US Vice-President Dan Quayle

- 'Our strength is we don't have any weaknesses. Our weakness is that we don't have any real strengths.'

  College football coach Frank Broyles

——— USELESS THINGS PEOPLE SAY ———

- 'We don't necessarily discriminate. We simply exclude certain types of people.'

  US colonel Gerald Wellman

- 'The people in the navy look on motherhood as being compatible with being a woman.'

  Rear Admiral James R Hogg

- 'I have no political ambitions for myself or my children.'

  Former US Ambassador to Great Britain
  Joseph P Kennedy, 1936

- 'He's a guy who gets up at six o'clock in the morning regardless of what time it is.'

  Boxing trainer Lou Duva

- 'God's wounds! I will pull down my breeches and they shall also see my arse.'

  King James I – when told the public wished to see him

- 'Who the hell wants to hear actors talk?'

  Warner Brothers, 1927

- 'It's like when I buy a horse. I don't want a thick neck and short legs.'

  Mickey Rourke – on his ideal woman

——— **USELESS THINGS PEOPLE SAY** ———

- 'If people get a kick out of running down pedestrians, you have to let them do it.'

  Video-game director Paul Jacobs

- 'He dribbles a lot and the opposition don't like it. You can see it all over their faces.'

  'I would not say David Ginola is the best left-winger in the Premiership, but there are none better.'

  Ron Atkinson

- 'I have been trained in private never to show emotion in public.'

  The Queen

- 'Solutions are not the answer.'

  US President Richard Nixon

- 'Happiness is good health and a bad memory.'

  Ingrid Bergman

- 'We live above the shop.'

  Prince Philip

- 'He treats us like men. He lets us wear earrings.'

  Houston sportsman Tonin Polk

USELESS THINGS PEOPLE SAY

- 'The object of war is not to die for your country but to make the other bastard die for his.'

  General George Patton

- 'The art world thinks of me as an uncultured, polo-playing clot.'

  Prince Philip

- 'During the scrimmage Tarkanian paced the sideline with his hands in his pockets while biting his nails.'

  Associated Press report

- 'I'm all in favour of keeping dangerous weapons out of the hands of fools. Let's start with typewriters.'

  US architect Frank Lloyd Wright

- 'Next up is the Central African Republic, located in Central Africa.'

  Australian sports commentator Bob Costas

- 'China is a big country, inhabited by many Chinese.'

  French President Charles de Gaulle

- 'Morcelli has four fastest 1,500-metre times ever. And all those times are at 1,500 metres.'

  Sports commentator David Coleman

———— USELESS THINGS PEOPLE SAY ————

● 'I deny the allegations and I deny the alligators.'

Chicago alderman when indicted

● 'Sit by the homely girl, you'll look better by comparison.'

Miss America 1983 – Debra Maffett

● 'God gave men both a penis and a brain, but unfortunately not enough blood supply to run both at the same time.'

Robin Williams, commenting on the Clinton sex scandal

● 'If everything seems under control, you're just not going fast enough.'

Grand Prix legend Mario Andretti

● 'Strangely, in slow-motion replay, the ball seemed to hang in the air for even longer.'

Sports commentator David Acfield

● 'I think "Hail to the Chief" has a nice ring to it.'

John F Kennedy – when asked to name his favourite song

● 'I have as much privacy as a goldfish in a bowl.'

Princess Margaret

——— USELESS THINGS PEOPLE SAY ———

- 'I don't want to achieve immortality through my work; I want to achieve immortality through not dying.'

  Woody Allen

- 'A period novel about the civil war? Who needs the civil war now? Who cares?'

  Pictorial Review editor when offered Gone with the Wind serialisation in 1936

- 'Boxing is all about getting the job done as quickly as possible, whether it takes 10 or 15 or 20 rounds.'

  Frank Bruno

- 'Models are like baseball players. We make a lot of money quickly, but all of a sudden we're 30 years old, we don't have a college education, we're qualified for nothing, and we're used to a very nice lifestyle. The best thing is to marry a movie star.'

  Supermodel Cindy Crawford

- 'I'm living so far beyond my income that we may almost be said to be living apart.'

  US poet E E Cummings

- 'If I were two-faced, would I be wearing this one?'

  Abraham Lincoln

——— USELESS THINGS PEOPLE SAY ———

● 'If you haven't got anything nice to say about anybody,
   come sit next to me.'

   Alice Roosevelt Longworth

● 'The Queen's [Victoria's] bosom has been deliciously
   handled and has been brought out by the artist in full
   rotundity.'

   The Times art critic

● 'The monarchy exists, not for its own benefit, but for
   that of the country. We don't come here for our health.
   We can think of better ways of enjoying ourselves.'

   Prince Philip – touring Canada

● 'I owe a lot to my parents, especially my mother and
   father.'

   Golfer Greg Norman

● 'You guys pair up in groups of three, then line
   up in a circle.'
   'Men, I want you just thinking of one word all season.
   One word and one word only. Super Bowl.'
   'You guys have to run a little more than full speed
   out there.'
   'You guys line up alphabetically by height.'

   Florida State football coach Bill Peterson

——— USELESS THINGS PEOPLE SAY ———

● 'Tragedy is when I cut my finger. Comedy is when you walk into an open sewer and die.'

Actor Mel Brooks

● 'He who hesitates is a damned fool.'

Mae West

● 'Isn't it a pity that Louis XVI was sent to the scaffold?'

Prince Philip – to a French Minister

● 'I don't feel we did wrong in taking this great country away from them. There were great numbers of people who needed new land, and the Indians were selfishly trying to keep it to themselves.'

John Wayne

● 'When I'm a blonde I can say the world is purple, and they'll believe me because they weren't listening to me.'

Actress Kylie Bax

● 'Everywhere I go I'm asked if I think the university stifles writers. My opinion is that they don't stifle enough of them.'

US novelist Flannery O'Connor

——— USELESS THINGS PEOPLE SAY ———

- 'If you are going through hell, keep going.'

  Sir Winston Churchill

- 'I say no to drugs. But they don't listen.'

  Singer Marilyn Manson

- 'Now, the only thing that remains unresolved is the resolution of the problem.'

  Ontario State Minister Thomas Wells

- 'It's a pleasant change to be in a country that isn't ruled by its people.'

  Prince Philip – to Paraguay's Dictator

- 'In the end, we will remember not the words of our enemies, but the silence of our friends.'

  Martin Luther King Jr

- 'The only happy artist is a dead artist, because only then you can't change. After I die, I'll probably come back as a paintbrush.'

  Sylvestor Stallone

- 'Assassins!'

  Italian conductor Arturo Toscanini, speaking to his orchestra

———— USELESS THINGS PEOPLE SAY ————

● 'Listen, everyone is entitled to my opinion.'

Madonna

● 'Never refuse an invitation to take the weight off your feet and seize every opportunity you can to relieve yourself.'

King George V's advice to the future King Edward VIII

● 'Too many pieces of music finish too long after the end.'

Igor Stravinsky

● 'She's more royal than the rest of us.'

The Queen – about Princess Michael

● 'There are only two tragedies in life: one is not getting what one wants, and the other is getting it.'

Oscar Wilde

● 'After finding no qualified candidates for the position of principal, the school board is extremely pleased to announce the appointment of David Steele to the post.'

Rhode Island Superintendent of Schools

● 'My advice to you is get married: if you find a good wife you'll be happy; if not, you'll become a philosopher.'

Socrates

—— USELESS THINGS PEOPLE SAY ——

● 'A verbal contract is not worth the paper it's written on.'
Samuel Goldwyn

● 'He's been around for a while and he's pretty old. He's 35 years old. That will give you some idea of how old he is.'
Broadcaster Ron Fairley

● 'The President has kept all of the promises he intended to keep.'
Clinton aide George Stephanopolous

● 'What will you do when you leave football, Jack? Will you stay in football?'
Stuart Hall, BBC Radio 5

● 'She ought to get a good whipping.'
Queen Victoria – about a suffragette

● 'I hope to God that he breaks his bloody neck.'
Prince Philip – about a press cameraman's accident

● 'Traffic is very heavy at the moment, so if you are thinking of leaving now, you'd better set off a few minutes earlier.'
Dublin radio reporter

—— USELESS THINGS PEOPLE SAY ——

● 'You know the one thing that's wrong with this country? Everyone gets a chance to have their fair say.'
US President Bill Clinton

● 'Smoking kills. If you're killed you've lost a very important part of your life.'
Brooke Shields during anti-smoking campaign

● 'Better make it six, I can't eat eight.'
Baseball player Dan Osinski – when asked how many slices he wanted his pizza cut into

● 'I love California. I practically grew up in Phoenix.'
US Vice-President Dan Quayle

● 'Which are the monkeys?'
Prince Philip – confronted by apes and journalists in Gibraltar

● 'Forgive your enemies, but never forget their names.'
John F Kennedy

● 'Armstrong Jones may be good at something – but it's nothing we teach here.'
Lord Snowdon's school report

---------- **USELESS THINGS PEOPLE SAY** ----------

● 'The streets are safe in Philadelphia. It's only the people who make them unsafe.'

> *Ex-Police Chief Frank Rizzo*

● 'Wishing myself in my sweetheart's arms, whose pretty dukkys I trust shortly to kiss.'

> *King Henry VIII – in a letter to Anne Boleyn*

● 'There is no housing shortage in Lincoln today. Just a rumour that is put about by people who have nowhere to live.'

> *Mayor of Lincoln G L Murfin*

● 'I have opinions of my own, strong opinions, but I don't always agree with them.'

> *President George Bush*

● 'And now will you all stand and be recognised.'

> *Texas House Speaker Gib Lewis to crowd in wheelchairs on Disability Day*

● 'I don't mind praying to the eternal father, but I must be the only man in the country afflicted with an eternal mother.'

> *The future King Edward VII – about Queen Victoria*

——— USELESS THINGS PEOPLE SAY ———

- 'I've always thought that underpopulated countries in Africa are vastly underpopulated.'

  World Bank chief economist Lawrence Summers

- 'It's the best way of wasting money that I know of.'

  Prince Philip – about the American moon shot

- 'From the moment I picked your book up until I laid it down I was convulsed with laughter. Some day I intend reading it.'

  Groucho Marx

- 'You dress like a cad. You act like a cad. You are a cad. Get out!'

  King George V – to his son, the future King Edward VIII

- 'Facts are stupid things.'

  US President Ronald Reagan

- 'A bachelor's life is no life for a single man.'

  Samuel Goldwyn

- 'I was provided with additional input that was radically different from the truth. I assisted in furthering that version.'

  Colonel Oliver North – testifying on Iran-Contra

——— USELESS THINGS PEOPLE SAY ———

● 'My presstitutes.'

Prince Andrew – about journalists

● 'Being pregnant is the occupational hazard of being a wife.'

Princess Anne

● 'Except for his car he's the only man on the track.'
'The lead car is absolutely unique, except for the one behind it, which is identical.'

Sports commentator Murray Walker

● 'If I had a choice of having a woman in my arms or shooting a bad guy on a horse, I'd take the horse. It's a lot more fun.'

Actor Kevin Costner

● 'I am not well. Pray get me a glass of brandy.'

King George IV – in reaction to meeting his arranged bride

● 'I am ready to meet my Maker. Whether my Maker is prepared for the great ordeal of meeting me is another matter.'

Sir Winston Churchill

● 'A miserly martinet with an insatiable sexual appetite.'

Prince Frederick – on his father, King George III

USELESS THINGS PEOPLE SAY

● 'False, lying, cowardly, nauseous puppy. The greatest ass, liar and beast in the world.'

> *King George III – on his eldest son, Prince Frederick*

● 'I wish the ground would open up this minute and sink the monster into the lowest hole in hell.'

> *Queen Caroline – on her eldest son, Prince Frederick*

● 'Oh doctor, can I have no more fun in bed?'

> *Queen Victoria – after her doctor's advice to have no more children*

● 'He has all the virtues I dislike and none of the vices I admire.'

> *Sir Winston Churchill*

● 'Marriage is the last decision on which I would want my head to be ruled by my heart.'

> *Prince Charles*

● 'His previous wives just didn't understand him.'

> *Mickey Rooney's eighth wife, Jan Chamberlein*

● 'The world is more like it is now than it ever was before.'

> *US President Dwight D Eisenhower*

────── USELESS THINGS PEOPLE SAY ──────

● 'I won't knight buggers.'

King George V – about homosexuals

● 'Every drop of blood in my veins is German.'

King Edward VIII

● 'If we don't succeed we run the risk of failure.'
'It is wonderful to be here in the great state of Chicago.'
'Illegitimacy is something we should talk about in terms
of not having.'
'It's time for the human race to enter the solar system.'
'It isn't pollution that is hurting the environment, it's the
impurities in our air and water that are doing it.'
'What a waste it is to lose one's mind. Or not to have a
mind is being very wasteful. How true that is.'

US Vice-President Dan Quayle

● 'It was more like being kidnapped.'

Princess Margaret – on her visit to Morocco

● 'There is only one Jesus Christ. All the rest is a dispute
over trifles.'

Queen Elizabeth I – on religion

● 'He will be known for a long time because of me.'

Duchess of Windsor – about the Duke

——— USELESS THINGS PEOPLE SAY ———

- 'I haven't committed a crime. All I did was fail to comply with the law.'

  New York Mayor David Dinkins – on failing to pay taxes

- 'I didn't know "Onward Christian Soldiers" was a Christian song.'

  Texas politician Aggie Pate

- 'He's passé. Nobody cares about Mickey any more. There are whole batches of Mickeys we just can't give away. I think we should phase him out!'

  Roy Disney to brother Walt, 1937

- 'What did you do about peeing?'

  King George V – to Charles Lindbergh after he flew the Atlantic solo

- 'I love Mickey Mouse more than any woman I have ever known.'

  Walt Disney

- 'The Supreme Court rules that murderers shall not be electrocuted twice for the same crime.'

  Cleveland Daily News headline

8

PEOPLE

PEOPLE

- To thank actor Harrison Ford for narrating a documentary, the London Museum of Natural History named a spider after him called *Calponia Harrisonfordi*.

- In the shower 75% of people wash from their tops to their bottoms.

- The world's tallest woman, Zeng Jinlian, from China, was 8 feet 1¾ inches (2 m 4.5 cm) tall.

- Oliver Cromwell was exhumed, hanged and decapitated two years after he died.

- The only woman in history to have married both a king of France and a king of England was Eleanor of Aquitane. Her husbands were Louis VII of France and Henry II of England.

- The last Ranee of Sarawak, who selected mistresses for her husband, the Raja, boasted that he had only ever rejected one of her choices.

- Attila the Hun died of a nosebleed on his wedding night in AD 453.

PEOPLE

- The 'new' bridal extra, which Wallis Simpson wore to her wedding with Edward VIII, was a gold coin, which she carried in her left shoe. It had been minted for Edward's coronation.

- Fleet commanders in the Pacific Theatre of war in World War II, Admiral Isoroku Yamamoto for the Japanese and Admiral Chester Nimitz for the United States, were each missing two fingers as a result of accidents while young officers on board ship.

- William Wrigley gave away free packs of chewing gum to customers who bought his baking powder. He soon abandoned the baking powder when he discovered they were buying it in order to get his gum.

- The word 'feminism' was misspelled 'feminisim' on the May/June 1996 cover of *Ms Magazine*.

- John Wilkes Booth shot President Lincoln in a theatre and was found in a warehouse. Lee Harvey Oswald shot President Kennedy from a warehouse and was found in a theatre.

- Cleopatra used squeezed pomegranate seeds for lipstick

PEOPLE

- The Scottish name Campbell actually means 'crooked mouth' in Gaelic.

- Teddy Roosevelt was so keen on boxing he had a boxing ring installed in the White House.

- Everybody's tongue print is unique.

- To celebrate his 700th parachute jump Flight Sergeant Hector Macmillan made his descent in full national Scottish dress while playing 'The Road to the Isles' on the bagpipes.

- People become sick a great deal more by staying indoors than by going out in the cold.

- There are more psychoanalysts in Buenos Aires, Argentina, than in any other city in the world.

- The car-making Dodge brothers, Horace and John, were Jewish, which is why the first Dodge emblem had a Star of David in it.

- A survey of career women who chose tattoos revealed that they preferred to adorn their left breast rather than their right breast by a ratio of three to one.

PEOPLE

- Richard Millhouse Nixon's name contains all the letters from the word 'criminal'. He was the first US president to have this distinction. The second was William Jefferson Clinton.

- US President Lyndon Johnson's family all shared the initials 'LBJ'. They were: Lyndon Baines Johnson, Lady Bird Johnson, Linda Bird Johnson and Lucy Baines Johnson. His dog was Little Beagle Johnson.

- Wartime President Franklin D Roosevelt was the first to have a presidential aircraft. He only flew on the specially equipped Douglas DC4, nicknamed 'the sacred cow', once – to travel to Yalta for the conference with Stalin and Churchill. The plane was fitted with a lift so he could board it in his wheelchair.

- Actor Laurence Oliver – later Lord Olivier – once called a press conference just to complain about service on British Rail. He was furious that kippers had been dropped from the menu.

- As the result of a duel being fought before becoming president, Andrew Jackson spent his adult life with a bullet no more than two inches (5 cm) away from his heart.

PEOPLE

- The dog that shared the bed of Napoleon and Josephine was called Fortune.

- At night the average person is about a quarter of an inch (0.6 cm) taller.

- Of the 102 people on board the *Mayflower* ten of them were called John.

- Henry Ford never had a driving licence.

- Before he discovered his real vocation as a lover and libertine, Casanova was preparing for the priesthood.

- US President Andrew Jackson's pet parrot had to be removed from his funeral in 1845 because it was swearing.

- King Louis XIV reigned for 72 years. He acceded to the throne at the age of five in 1643. He once declared: 'L'Etat? C'est moi' – I am the State.

- Only one person in two billion will live to be 116 years old or over.

- Elizabeth I of England suffered from anthophobia – a fear of roses.

PEOPLE

- Ian Lewis of Standish, Lancashire, England, spent 30 years tracing his family history and contacting 2,000 distant relatives before discovering he was adopted as a one-month-old baby.

- Humans spend almost a third of their lives in bed.

- When asked what he thought of Western civilisation, Mahatma Gandhi replied: 'I think it would be a good idea.'

- The Roman emperor Nero, whose father was dead and mother in exile, was brought up by a barber and a male ballet dancer.

- Abraham Lincoln's mother died after drinking milk from the family cow, which had eaten poisonous mushrooms.

- Stalin's real name was Iosif Vissarionovich Dzhugashvili. He began using the pseudonym Stalin, meaning 'Man of Steel', in 1936.

- Two presidential families had their own way of preventing their conversations being overheard by White House guests or staff. The Hoovers spoke to each other in Chinese. The Coolidge family spoke in sign language.

---------------------------------- **PEOPLE** ----------------------------------

- The famous scar that earned Al Capone his nickname of 'Scarface' was inflicted by the brother of a girl he had insulted. The boy attacked him with a knife leaving him with the three distinctive scars.

- Because snow is relatively unknown on the continent of Africa, children there know the fairytale heroine as 'Flower White' rather than as Snow White.

- Mexican revolutionary Sancho Villa's dying words were: 'Don't let it end like this. Tell them I said something.'

- People start to shrink after the age of 30.

- When George Washington was US President there were only some 350 federal employees.

- There were six rulers of Egypt named Cleopatra before the woman who became linked with Julius Caesar and Mark Anthony.

- French statesman Cardinal Richelieu would jump over the furniture every morning as his daily exercise routine.

- Sir Walter Raleigh had a black greyhound called Hamlet.

PEOPLE

- The world's tallest man was an American, Robert Wadlo, who was eight feet eleven inches tall.

- Queen Victoria had a sprig of holly placed below her collar as a child to train her to keep her chin up.

- The Prince of Wales, later to become Edward VIII, was saved from arrest during a police Prohibition raid by singer Texas Guinan, who pushed him into her nightclub kitchen and gave him a chef's hat and skillet.

- After Egypt's King Farouk was overthrown by Gamal Nasser, he predicted that one day there would be only five kings left in the world – the kings of Hearts, Spades, Diamonds, Clubs and England.

- Children grow faster in springtime than at any other time of year.

- Captain William Bligh, of the *Mutiny on the Bounty* fame, was thrown out after another mutiny almost 20 years after that event. While he was governor of New South Wales, in 1808, British army officers captured him and forced him to resign. He had tried to stop the colony's rum trade.

PEOPLE

- In 1946, to celebrate Aga Khan's 60 years as leader of the Ismaili Sect of the Shiite Muslims, his followers gave his weight in diamonds. He weighed 243¼ lb (111 kg).

- Queen Anne's bow legs inspired a furniture style.

- In his various palaces the French King Louis XIV had 413 beds.

- During his time as president William Taft had a bathtub big enough to hold four normal men installed in the White House in order to accommodate his massive 23-stone (146.06-kg) figure.

- Violet Gibson Burns typed continuously at her typewriter for 264 hours – a world record.

- England's King Henry VI was only nine months old when he acceded to the throne.

- When Imelda Marcos and her deposed Filipino husband, President Ferdinand Marcos, went into exile in 1986, she left behind 2,400 pairs of size 8 ½ shoes.

- In the eight-year period Ronald Reagan was president, the White House bought 12 tons of his favourite jelly beans.

PEOPLE

- Every night Cleopatra had her mattress stuffed with rose petals.

- Lyndon Johnson was obsessed with secrecy. He usually wrote 'burn this', even on his personal mail.

- During the eleven-month-long African hunting expedition that followed Theodore Roosevelt's term as president in 1909, he shot 296 animals including nine lions and five elephants.

- Eight of America's presidents were born British subjects.

- President Lyndon Johnson called his pet beagles Him and Her. President Franklin D Roosevelt and wife Eleanor called their pistols, which they kept under their pillows, His and Hers.

- Before founding the Russian communist party and becoming Premier of the first Soviet Government, Lenin lived in exile in England, under the name of Jacob Richter.

- Joan of Arc was only nineteen years of age when she was burned at the stake.

PEOPLE

- George Washington named his three foxhounds Drunkard, Tippler and Tipsy.

- Cleopatra was only twelve years old when she took her first lover.

- English haberdasher James Hetherington was arrested in 1797 when he wore a silk top hat for the first time in London. The charge read that he was guilty of wearing a 'tall structure of shining lustre calculated to disturb the people'.

- Romans had three words to describe kisses: the kiss for acquaintances, the *basium*; the kiss between close friends, the *osculum*; and the kiss between lovers, the *suavium*.

- When President Lincoln's widow Mary Todd Lincoln was declared insane in 1875, doctors found $56,000 worth of bonds concealed in her underwear.

- In 1512 Louis XII of France ordered the removal of all the garbage, which for years had been routinely thrown over the walls of Paris. He did it not for hygienic reasons, but because an enemy might scale the garbage to climb over the walls.

PEOPLE

- In the Masters and Johnson study the man with the longest penis was just five feet seven inches tall.

- The average clerk produces 4.6 lb (2 kg) of waste paper a day.

- More than half the world's population still rely on their own or their animals' muscles for all their power.

- The fashion of women having their nipples pierced to wear gold or jewelled pins or rings is not a new one. It began in England around 1890.

- In 1841 in England a third of the men and half the women who married signed the register with a mark rather than their written names.

- Louis XIV France took only three baths during his 77-year lifetime: one when he was baptised; one at the insistence of one of his mistresses; and the last when a doctor lanced a boil on his bottom and ordered him to soak it in a tub of hot water.

- In the early days of Hollywood, western sets were made to seven-eighths scale to make the heroes seem larger.

——————————— **PEOPLE** ———————————

- Cambridge students were not allowed to keep dogs in their rooms. Lord Byron kept a bear.

9

SEVENS

SEVENS

- *The Magnificent Seven*
  Charles Bronson – Bernordo
  Yul Brynner – Chris
  Horst Buchholz – Chico
  James Coburn – Britt
  Brad Dexter – Harry
  Steve McQueen – Vin
  Robert Vaughn – Lee

- The Seven Dwarfs
  Bashful
  Doc
  Dopey
  Grumpy
  Happy
  Sleepy
  Sneezy

- The Seven Deadly Sins
  Avarice
  Envy
  Gluttony
  Lust
  Pride
  Sloth
  Wrath

SEVENS

- The Seven Wonders of the Ancient World
  Pyramids of Giza
  Hanging Gardens of Babylon
  Mausoleum of Halicarnassus
  Temple of Artemis at Ephesus
  Colossus of Rhodes
  Pharos (Lighthouse) of Alexandria
  Statue of Zeus at Olympia

- The Seven Virtues
  Justice
  Fortitude
  Prudence
  Temperance
  Faith
  Hope
  Charity

- The Seven Seas
  North Atlantic Ocean
  South Atlantic Ocean
  North Pacific Ocean
  South Pacific Ocean
  Indian Ocean
  Arctic Ocean
  Antarctic Ocean

SEVENS

- The Seven Sizes of Grand Piano
  Baby Grand – 5 ft 8 inches
  Living Room Grand – 5 ft 10 inches
  Professional Grand – 6 ft
  Drawing Room Grand – 6 ft 4 inches
  Parlour Grand – 6 ft 8 inches
  Half Concert Grand – 7 ft 4 inches
  Concert Grand – 8 ft 11 inches or longer

- The Seven Children of Baron von Trapp of
  The Sound of Music fame
  Liesel
  Friedrich
  Louisa
  Brigitta
  Kurt
  Marta
  Gretl

- The Seven Colours of the Rainbow
  Red
  Orange
  Yellow
  Green
  Blue
  Indigo
  Violet

SEVENS

- The Seven Days of Creation
  Created heaven and earth; day and night.
  Divided heaven from earth.
  Created the land, the sea and vegetation.
  Created the sun, the moon and the stars.
  Created creatures great and small.
  Created mankind.
  Sanctified the seventh day as the day of rest.

- The Seven Hills of Rome
  Palatine
  Capitoline
  Quirinal
  Viminal
  Esquiline
  Caelian
  Aventine

- The Seven Ages of Man (according to Shakespeare)
  The Infant
  The Schoolboy
  The Lover
  The Soldier
  The Justice
  The Pantaloon
  The Second Childhood

SEVENS

- From 1940 to 1962, Bing Crosby and Bob Hope made seven road movies. The seven destinations were:
  Rio
  Hong Kong
  Singapore
  Zanzibar
  Morocco
  Utopia
  Bali

- The Seven Ionian Islands
  Corfu
  Cephalonia
  Zacynthus
  Leucas
  Ithaca
  Cythera
  Paxos

- The Seven Medieval Champions of Christendom
  St George – England
  St Denis – France
  St James – Spain
  St Anthony – Italy
  St Andrew – Scotland
  St Patrick – Ireland
  St David – Wales

— SEVENS —

- The Seven Gifts of the Holy Spirit
  Wisdom
  Understanding
  Counsel
  Fortitude
  Knowledge
  Piety
  Fear of the Lord

- The Seven Sisters

- The seven stars in the Taurus constellation visible to the naked eye, named after the daughters of the Titan Atlas and the Oceanid Pleione in Greek mythology:
  Alcyone
  Maia
  Electra
  Merope
  Taygete
  Celaeno
  Asterope

10

ODDS AND ENDS

ODDS AND ENDS

- America's Internal Revenue Service employees' tax manual has instructions for collecting taxes after a nuclear war.

- The only wood ever used by renowned English cabinet-maker Thomas Chippendale was mahogany.

- The typing exercise 'Now is the time for all good men to come to the aid of the party' was created by Charles E Weller.

- A year is exactly 365 days 5 hours 48 minutes and 46 seconds long.

- Khaki was first adopted for military uniforms in 1880 in the Afghan war. Only then was it finally admitted it was the best camouflage colour.

- In an amazing demonstration, crack shot Annie Oakley, using an ordinary rifle, once shot at 5,000 pennies, tossed into the air one after the other, and hit an incredible 4,777, giving her a 96% success rate.

- A bear was the first creature to test an ejection seat from a supersonic aircraft in 1962. It was ejected at 35,000 ft (10,668 m) and made a safe descent by parachute.

ODDS AND ENDS

- The average lifespan of a Stone Age caveman was eighteen years.

- *Playboar Magazine* has a centrefold that features the littermate of the month.

- In 1970 the Procrastinators' Club of America demanded a full refund for the Liberty Bell from London's Whitechapel Foundry because it had cracked in 1835. The foundry graciously agreed – provided the defective item could be returned in its original packaging.

- The words 'atomic bomb' were coined by H G Wells in his science-fiction story *The World Set Free*, written in 1914.

- The rocket launch countdown from ten to one stemmed from a 1928 German silent movie, *The Girl in the Moon*, in which director Fritz Lang reversed the count to build suspense.

- More diamonds are bought for Christmas (31%) than for any other event of the year.

- The average suit of armour for a medieval knight weighed between 50 and 55 lb (23–25 kg).

ODDS AND ENDS

- The highest wind speed every recorded on earth was in New Hampshire, in the United States, on 24 April 1934. It was 231 mph (372 kph).

- If all the water was removed from the body of an average 160 lb (73 kg) man there would be just 64 lb (29 kg) of corpse left.

- Until 153BC New Year's Day fell in March. The Romans then switched to starting the New Year on 1 January.

- Supermodel Cindy Crawford was valedictorian of her high-school class and won a full college scholarship to study chemical engineering at Northwestern University in Evanston, Illinios. She dropped out after one term to take up a career in modelling.

- The Greek philosopher Socrates was trained as a stone cutter.

- Hugh Hefner's all-black private jet was named Big Bunny.

- In his New Year's Day column US journalist Westbrook Pegler repeated the same sentence 50 times. It was: 'I will never mix gin, beer and whiskey again.'

ODDS AND ENDS

- When Winston Churchill learned that Hitler had dubbed his country home Eagle's Nest he called his English country home Chartwell 'Cosy Pig'.

- The life expectancy of a modern toilet is 50 years.

- The first man to use the phrase 'The bigger they are the harder they fall' was heavyweight boxer Bob Fitzsimmons. He was talking of champion James J Jeffries, whom he fought in 1902. Fitzsimmons lost.

- British seaman James Bartley was swallowed alive by a whale in 1891 and survived for two days in its stomach before being released by his shipmates. He lived another 35 years to tell the tale.

- The idea of flying a flag at half-mast as a sign of mourning came from the navy, where the top of the mast would be left empty for the invisible flag of death during a funeral at sea in the seventeenth century. The standard flag would be lowered to leave the mast top empty.

- The Nobel Peace Prize medal depicts three naked men with their hands on each other's shoulders.

ODDS AND ENDS

- Buckingham Palace in London has more than 600 rooms.

- There are 412 doors in the White House.

- The first country to impose a general income tax was Britain, in 1799. It was done as a temporary measure to finance the war against Napoleon.

- Clocks made before 1687 only had an hour hand.

- The making of bottle caps in the United States uses more steel production than is used in building motor-car bodies.

- The Boston University bridge is the only place in the world where a boat can sail under a train driving under a car driving under an aeroplane.

- When a waitress in America draws a happy face on a meal bill her tips go up by 18%. If a waiter does the same, his tips rise by only 3% on average.

- On a Sunday in Salt Lake City, Utah, you can be fined up to £1,000 (about $1,600) for whistling.

ODDS AND ENDS

- When Hitler announced the founding of the Third Reich he declared the first two to have been the Holy Roman Empire of Charlemagne and the second the German Empire founded by Bismarck in 1871.

- The average soldier in World War I was three-quarters of an inch (2 cm) shorter than the average soldier in World War II.

- The first ever world summit on 'toilets' was held in Singapore in November 2001.

- The brain of Neanderthal man was bigger than that of modern man.

- The Hoochinoo Indians provided the nickname 'Hooch' for alcohol. They produced an incredibly strong liquor that knocked people senseless.

- The watermelon-seed-spitting world record is 65 ft 4 inches (20 m 10 cm).

- A pin-up photo of film star Rita Hayworth was stuck to the first atomic bomb to be tested on the Bikini atoll, in the western Pacific, in 1946.

ODDS AND ENDS

- The only inanimate symbol in the zodiac is Libra – the scales.

- By the time they are twenty years of age the average Western person has been exposed to over one million television commercials.

- Ninety-six per cent of all women think that all toilets should be cleaned once a week.

- The abbreviation AD (Anno Domini), the year of our Lord, should properly be placed in front of the year – thus 500 BC but AD 2003.

- At the battle of Waterloo Napoleon's white horse was called Marengo and Wellington rode the chestnut Copenhagen. They were named after the two men's famous victories.

- One in every six guns in the world is an AK-47.

- The longest flight every recorded of a propane explosion was when a railroad tanker car was thrown 3,000 ft (914 m) after it exploded during a train crash in Illinois, US. It also demolished a steel tower in its path.

ODDS AND ENDS

- British royalty is rather slow to catch up with the modern world. Foreign ambassadors are still described as 'Ambassadors to the Court of St James', which was the royal palace before Buckingham Palace was built.

- To fall over, a bowling pin need only tilt 7.5°.

- The 'v' (versus) in the name of a court case does not stand for versus but for 'and' in civil proceedings or 'against' in criminal proceedings.

- 14 February was declared St Valentine's Day in AD 498 by Pope Gelasius.

- Oak trees do not bear acorns until they are at least 50 years old.

- The volume of the moon is the same volume as that of the Pacific Ocean.

- More beer than water was taken aboard the *Mayflower* before the Pilgrim Fathers set off on their epic journey from England.

- Hara-kiri is an impolite way of saying the Japanese word '*seppuku*' which literally means 'belly-splitting'.

ODDS AND ENDS

- Mantles of gas lanterns are radioactive and will set off an alarm at a nuclear reactor.

- Mexico once had three presidents in one day.

- People who are more educated are more likely to drink alcohol.

- In Moscow the skating rinks cover more than 250,000 sq. m of land during the winter.

- Presbyterians is an anagram of Britney Spears.

- Twenty-one per cent of American smokers do not believe that nicotine is addictive.

- In the London telephone directory the House of Lords comes between the House of Leather and the House of Love.

- Packard was the first motor-car company to replace the steering tiller with the steering wheel in 1900.

- It was a dentist who invented the electric chair.

ODDS AND ENDS

- George Washington, a four-star general in his lifetime, was posthumously promoted to six-star general of the armies of congress by US President Jimmy Carter, who said America's first president should also be the highest-ranking military official.

- According to the Holy Days and Fasting Days Act of 1551 every British citizen must attend a Christian church service on Christmas Day and must not use any kind of vehicle to get to the service. The law has never been repealed.

- The average parent typically spends only nine minutes playing with their children on Christmas morning.

- A quarter of the bones in your body are in your feet.

- Shang Sung turned a single piece of dough into 8,192 noodles in under a minute in Singapore on 31 July 1994.

- An average human produces enough saliva in a lifetime to fill two standard-sized swimming pools.

- Coconuts kill more people in the world each year than sharks do. Sharks kill about 150 and coconuts kill some 2,000.

ODDS AND ENDS

- It is an offence in Britain, with up to a five-year jail sentence, to riotously demolish a hovel.

- Charlie Brown would be four and a half feet (about one metre) tall if he were a real person. His head would take up 2 ft (0.6 m) of this.

- The most popular car colour in the world is red.

- The average acre of corn contains 7.2 million kernels.

- The cigarette lighter was invented before the match.

- The full, official, name of Jesus College, Cambridge, is 'The College of the Holy Trinity and the most Blessed and Exalted Virgin St Radegund'.

- Only seven prisoners were liberated when the Bastille was stormed in 1789 at the start of the French Revolution.

- When the atomic bomb exploded on Hiroshima, 61,825 homes were destroyed.

- Marlboro's first owner died of lung cancer.

ODDS AND ENDS

- The snapping turtle, which eats carrion, is used by police in some countries to find dead bodies in lakes, ponds and swamps.

- The film star who achieved the highest military rank ever was James Stewart who became a brigadier general.

- Fifteen per cent of women in the United States send themselves flowers on Valentine's Day.

- Police issue tickets for driving too slow on Germany's Autobahn.

- Tights became the best-selling leg covering for women after Mary Quant created the mini skirt in the 60s. The mini skirt demanded a leg covering that went all the way up to the bottom.

- In American military terminology a shovel is known as a 'combat emplacement evacuator'.

- If the whole population of China jumped up and down at the same time, the vibration could create a tidal wave that would engulf the United States.

--------------- **ODDS AND ENDS** ---------------

- The Daimler Conquest was named after its then price of £1,066.

- 'Jingle Bells' was originally written for Thanksgiving.

- Both General George Custer and Chief Crazy Horse of the Sioux Indians, protaganists at the Battle of the Little Bighorn, were called 'curly' as children.

- The smile is the only physical gesture that man does not share with other animals.

- Out of 2,250,000 pianos in Britain 1,800,000 of them are said to be out of tune at any given moment.

- Blackbeard the pirate would tuck slow-burning fuses under his tricorne hat – wreathing his head in black smoke – to frighten his opponents in battle.

- It is against the law to be a prostitute in Siena, Italy, if your name is Mary.

- There are an estimated 400,000 camels in Australia, descendants of the pack animals taken there in the nineteenth century, and some are exported to Saudi Arabia to provide food in restaurants.

——— ODDS AND ENDS ———

- In the sixteenth century the law in England allowed men to beat their wives – but only before 10 pm.

- 'Freelance' comes from the knights whose lances were free for hire and who were not pledged to one master.

- Medieval knights put shark's skin on their sword handles to give them a more secure grip. They would dig the shark's scales into their palms.

- In a recent year, of the 317 shootings by New York City police officers 27% of the victims were dogs.

- A full-grown pumpkin vine has an average fifteen miles (24 km) of roots.

- When George Washington was elected president there was a king in France, a czarina in Russia, an emperor in China and a shogun in Japan. Of these, only the presidency remains.

- It took Napoleon only four hours to send a message from Rome to Paris – almost 700 miles (1,127 km) – using a semaphore system from hilltop to hilltop.

ODDS AND ENDS

- Non-smokers dream more than smokers do.

- Grapes explode when heated in a microwave oven.

- In the four years from 1347 to 1351 the Black Death plague reduced the population of Europe by a third.

- A zarf is the holder of a handleless coffee cup.

- Revolvers cannot be fitted with silencers. The gases escape the cylinder gaps at the rear of the barrel and cannot be prevented from making a noise by a device fitted to the end of the barrel.

- Astronauts cannot cry in space because there is no gravity to assist the tear flow.

- Napoleon Bonaparte's official emblem was the bumblebee.

- The buzz generated by an electric razor in America is in the key of B flat.

- In the Ukraine a spider's web found on Christmas morning is supposed to bring good luck. For this reason an artificial spider and web is often the main tree decoration in Ukrainian homes.

ODDS AND ENDS

- Armoured knights would raise their visors to identify themselves when they rode past the king. This habit is the origin of the modern military salute.

- The Americans tried to train bats to drop bombs during World War II.

- The world's biggest bell is the Tsar Karokal, which weighs 216 tons (219,467 kg) and was cast in the Kremlin in 1733. It is cracked and cannot be rung.

- The first product to have a bar code was Wrigley's chewing gum.

- Benjamin Davis became the first ever black general in history in the US Army, in 1940. His son, Benjamin Davis Jr, became the first black general in history in the US Air Force, in 1954.

- To 'testify' was based on men in the Roman court guaranteeing a statement by swearing on their testicles.

- A hurricane releases more energy in ten minutes than all the nuclear weapons combined.

- Scotland exports sand to Saudi Arabia.

---------- **ODDS AND ENDS** ----------

- Moses, Charles Darwin, Aristotle and Sir Isaac Newton all had bad stutters.

- In his lifetime an average man will spend 3,350 hours shaving – or 139 ½ days.

- The names of the three wise monkeys are: Mizaru – see no evil; Mikazaru – hear no evil; and Mozaru – speak no evil.

- Until the late nineteenth century British sailors were forbidden to use forks as they were considered unmanly and harmful to discipline.

- If you cut a piece of paper in half, place the two pieces on top of each other and cut them in half again and again, until you have done it 60 times, the stack of paper will reach to the sun and back.

- Seventy per cent of household dust is dead skin cells.

- The top three cork-producing countries are Spain, Portugal and Algeria.

- Raindrops are not teardrop-shaped; they are rounded at the top and flat on the bottom.

ODDS AND ENDS

- Socks – first found in Egyptian tombs – remained popular for 5,000 years, until the fifteenth century and the introduction of tights.

- The toothbrush was invented in 1498.

- Pantalettes were designed in Victorian times to conceal limb areas not covered by skirts. Victorians even used them to cover table legs.

- Houdini actually trained his pet dog to escape from a miniature set of handcuffs.

- A coat hanger is 44 inches long if straightened.

- 4,000 people are injured by teapots every year.

- A 60-minute cassette contains 565 feet of tape.

- A dime has 118 ridges around the edge.

- A good quality Persian rug which contains one million knots in every three square inches can last as long as 500 years.

- A good typist can strike 20 keys in a second.

ODDS AND ENDS

- A person uses more household energy shaving with a hand razor at a sink (because of the water power, the water pump and so on) than he would by using an electric razor.

- A quarter has 119 rigdes on its edge.

- A toothpick is the object most often choked on by Americans.

- A typical double mattress contains as many as two million house dust mites.

- A wedding ring is generally exempt by law from inclusion among the assets in a bankruptcy estate. That means that a wedding ring can't be seized by creditors, no matter how much the bankrupt person owes.

- According to a market research survey done some time ago, 68 per cent of consumers receiving junk mail actually open the envelopes.

- According to one study, 24 per cent of lawns have some sort of lawn ornament.

- All hospitals in Singapore use Pampers nappies.

ODDS AND ENDS

- All 50 states are listed across the top of the Lincoln Memorial on the back of the American $5 bill.

- Aluminium is strong enough to support 90,000 pounds per square inch.

- Americans spend $1.5 billion dollars every year on toothpaste.

- Approximately 30 billion cakes of Ivory Soap had been manufactured by 1990.

- At the height of inflation in Germany in the early 1920s, one pound was equal to a quintillion German marks.

- Colgate faced a big obstacle marketing toothpaste in Spanish-speaking countries. Colgate translates into the command 'go hang yourself'.

- Cow is a Japanese brand of shaving foam.

- Each king in a deck of playing cards represents a great king from history. Spades – King David; Clubs – Alexander the Great; Hearts – Charlemagne; and Diamonds – Julius Caesar.

---------------------- **ODDS AND ENDS** ----------------------

- Each of the suits on a deck of cards represents the four major pillars of the economy in the middle ages: heart represented the Church; spades represented the military; clubs represented agriculture; and diamonds represented the merchant class.

- Each of us generate five pounds of rubbish a day; most of it is paper.

- Every year, over 8,800 people injure themselves with a toothpick.

- How valuable is the penny you found lying on the ground? If it takes just a second to pick it up a person could make £36.00 per hour just picking up pennies.

- If done perfectly, any Rubik's cube combination can be solved in 17 turns.

- If you lace your shoes from the inside to the outside, the fit will be snugger around your big toe.

- In 1955, one-third of all watches sold were Timexes.

- In 1977, Cairo only had 208,000 telephones and no telephone books.

ODDS AND ENDS

- In 1990, there were about 15,000 vacuum cleaner-related accidents in the US.

- In every deck of cards, the King of Hearts is sticking his sword through his head. That's why he's often called the Suicide King.

- In order for a deck of cards to be mixed up enough to play with properly, it should be shuffled at least seven times.

- It takes a plastic container 50,000 years to start decomposing.

- Ivory bar soap floating was a mistake. They had been mixing the soap formula causing excess air bubbles that made it float. Customers wrote and told how much they loved that it floated, and it has floated ever since.

- John F Kennedy's rocking chair was auctioned off for $442,000.

- Ketchup is excellent for cleaning brass, especially tarnished or corroded brass.

ODDS AND ENDS

- Kleenex tissues were originally used as filters in gas masks.

- Lang Martin balanced seven golf balls vertically without adhesive at Charlotte, NC on 9 February 1980.

- Mixing Sani-Flush and Comet cleaners has been known to cause explosions.

- More people use blue toothbrushes than red ones.

- Mosquito repellants do not repel. They hide you. The spray blocks the mosquito's sensors so they do not know you are there.

- Murphy's Oil Soap is the chemical most commonly used to clean elephants.

- No piece of paper can be folded in half more than seven times.

- On average, 100 people choke on ballpoint pens every year.

- On average, there are 333 squares of toilet paper on a roll.

ODDS AND ENDS

- On the new American hundred dollar bill the time on the clock tower of Independence Hall is 4:10.

- Playing cards became the first paper currency of Canada in 1685, when the French governor used them to pay off some war debts.

- Playing cards in India are round.

- Q-TIPS Cotton Swabs were originally called Baby Gays.

- Rubber bands last longer when refrigerated.

- Scotch tape has been used as an anti-corrosive shield on the Goodyear Blimp.

- Scotchgard is a combination of the words Scotch, meaning Scotsman, and a misspelling of guard, meaning to protect.

- Some Eskimos have been known to use refrigerators to keep their food from freezing.

- Some toothpastes contain antifreeze.

ODDS AND ENDS

- The Australian $5, $10, $20, $50 and $100 notes are made out of plastic.

- The average person looks at eight houses before buying one.

- The average lead pencil will draw a line 35 miles long or write approximately 50,000 English words.

- The average mouse pad is 8.75 inches by 7.5 inches.

- The average woman consumes six pounds of lipstick in her lifetime.

- The average women's handbag weighs three to five pounds.

- The dial tone of a normal telephone is in the key F.

- The end of a hammer, opposite the striking end, is called a peen.

- The face of a penny can hold thirty drops of water.

ODDS AND ENDS

- The first US coin to bear the words, 'United States of America' was a penny made in 1727. It was also inscribed with the plain-spoken motto: 'Mind your own business'.

- The holes in fly swatters are used to lower air resistance.

- The hundred billionth crayon made by Crayola was Perriwinkle Blue.

- The list of ingredients that make up lipstick include fish scales.

- The most popular contact lens colour is blue.

- The opposite sides of a dice cube add up to seven.

- The plastic things on the end of shoelaces are called aglets.

- The quartz crystal in your wristwatch vibrates 32,768 times a second.

- The Ramses brand condom is named after the great Pharaoh Rameses II who fathered over 160 children.

——— ODDS AND ENDS ———

- The side of a hammer is a cheek.

- Bill Bowerman, founder of Nike, got his first shoe idea after staring at a waffle iron. He got the idea of using squared spikes to make shoes lighter.

- Jeans were named after Genoa, Italy, where the first denim cloth was made.

- On average, most people button their shirts upwards.

- The armhole in clothing is called an armsaye.

- The bra Marilyn Monroe wore in the movie '*Some Like It Hot*', was sold for $14,000.

- The YKK on the zipper of your Levis stands for Yoshida Kogyo Kabushibibaisha, the world's largest zipper manufacturer.

- 40,000 Americans are injured by toilets every year.

- A flush toilet exists today that dates back to 2000 BC.

- About a third of people flush while they are still sitting on the toilet.

ODDS AND ENDS

- In 1825, the first toilet was installed in the White House.

- In true kingly fashion, Elvis passed away while sitting on the throne.

- Most toilets flush in E flat.

- Poet Henry Wadsworth Longfellow was the first American to have plumbing installed in his house in 1840.

- The first toilet ever seen on television was on *Leave it to Beaver*.

- The Soviet Sukhoi-34 is the first strike fighter with a toilet in it.

- Toilets in Australia flush counter clockwise.

- Ninety-four per cent of all households in Belgium with children up to the age of 14 years own LEGO products.

- Barbie's full name is Barbara Millicent Roberts.

- Barbie's measurements if she were life-size: 5 feet 9 inches tall, 33-18-31$\frac{1}{2}$.

---------------- **ODDS AND ENDS** ----------------

- If you took a standard slinky and stretched it out it would measure 87 feet.

- In 1980, Namco released PAC-MAN, the most popular video game (or arcade game) of all time. The original name was going to be PUCK MAN, but executives saw the potential for vandals to scratch out part of the P in the games marquee and labelling.

- It takes an average of 48 to 100 tries to solve a rubix cube puzzle.

- Slinkys were invented by an airplane mechanic; he was playing with engine parts and realized the possible secondary use of one of the springs.

- The hula hoop was the biggest selling toy in 1957.

- The yo-yo originated in the Phillippines, where it is used as a weapon in hunting.

- There are 42 dots on a pair of dice.

- There are more Barbie dolls in Italy than there are Canadians in Canada.

ODDS AND ENDS

● Totally Hair Barbie is the best selling Barbie of all time.

● When the divorce rate goes up in the United States, toy makers say the sale of toys also rises.

● A Virginia law requires all bathtubs to be kept out in the yards, not inside the house.

● According to a British law passed in 1845, attempting to commit suicide was a capital offence. Offenders could be hanged for trying.

● Christmas was once illegal in England.

● Duelling is legal in Paraguay as long as both parties are registered blood donors.

● In Alaska it is illegal to shoot at a moose from the window of an aeroplane or other flying vehicle.

● In Cleveland, Ohio it is illegal to catch mice without a hunting licence.

● In Italy, it is illegal to make coffins out of anything except nutshells or wood.

ODDS AND ENDS

- In England during Queen Victoria's reign, it was illegal to be a homosexual but not a lesbian. The reason being that when the Queen was approving the law she wouldn't believe that women would do that.

- In Sweden, while prostitution is legal, it is illegal for anyone to use the services of a prostitute.

- In Texas, it is illegal to put graffiti on someone else's cow.

- In Arizona, it is illegal to hunt camels.

- It is illegal, in Malaysia, for restaurants to substitute toilet paper as table napkins. Repeat offenders go to jail.

- Mailing an entire building has been illegal in the US since 1916 when a man mailed a 40,000-ton brick house across Utah to avoid high freight rates.

- Pennsylvania was the first colony to legalize witchcraft.

- A monkey was once tried and convicted for smoking a cigarette in South Bend, Indiana.

- Every citizen of Kentucky is required by law to take a bath at least once a year.

ODDS AND ENDS

- In Hartford, Connecticut, you may not, under any circumstances, cross the street walking on your hands.

- In Indiana, it is illegal to ride public transportation for at least 30 minutes after eating garlic.

- In Minnesota, it is illegal for woman to be dressed up as Santa Claus on city streets.

- In Morrisville, Pennsylvania, women need a legal permit before they can wear lipstick in public.

- In Kansas, it's against the law to catch fish with your bare hands.

- Under the law of Mississippi, there's no such thing as a female Peeping Tom.

- Adolf Hitler had planned to change the name of Berlin to Germania.

- Adolf Hitler refused to shake Jesse Owens' hand at the 1936 Olympics because he was black.

- Adolf Hitler was *Time's* Man of the Year for 1938.

ODDS AND ENDS

- Al Capone's brother was a town sheriff.

- Albert Einstein's last words were in German. Since the attending nurse did not understand German, his last words will never be known.

- Alexander Graham Bell never telephoned his wife or mother. They were both deaf.

- Alexander the Great was an epileptic.

- Alfred Hitchcock did not have a belly button.

- Aristotle thought that blood cooled the brain.

- Astronaut Buzz Aldrin's mother's maiden name was 'Moon'.

- Astronaut Neil Armstrong stepped on the moon with his left foot first.

- At a fair in Maine, a boy spit a watermelon seed 38 feet.

- At age 16, Confucius was a corn inspector.

ODDS AND ENDS

- Attila the Hun was a dwarf. Pepin the Short, Aesop, Gregory the Tours, Charles III of Naples and the Pasha Hussain were all less than 3.5 feet tall.

- At age 47, the Rolling Stones' bassist, Bill Wyman, began a relationship with 13-year-old Mandy Smith, with her mother's blessing. Six years later, they were married, but the marriage only lasted a year. Not long after, Bill's 30-year-old son Stephen married Mandy's mother, age 46. That made Stephen a stepfather to his former stepmother. If Bill and Mandy had remained married, Stephen would have been his father's father-in-law and his own grandpa.

- At age 90, Peter Mustafic of Botovo, Yugoslavia, suddenly began speaking again after a silence of 40 years. The Yugoslavian news agency quoted him as saying, 'I just didn't want to do military service, so I stopped speaking in 1920; then I got used to it'.

- Augustus Caesar had achluophobia – the fear of sitting in the dark.

- Benjamin Franklin wanted the turkey, not the eagle, to be the US national symbol.

ODDS AND ENDS

- Benjamin Franklin's peers did not give him the assignment of writing the Declaration of Independence because they feared that he would conceal a joke in it.

- British politician John Montagu, the 4t6h Earl of Sandwich, is credited with naming the sandwich. He developed the habit of eating beef between slices of toast so he could continue playing cards uninterrupted.

- Buzz Aldrin was the first man to pee his pants on the moon.

- Catherine de Medici was the first woman in Europe to use tobacco. She took it in a mixture of snuff.

- Charles de Gaulle's final words were 'It hurts'.

- Charles Dickens never finished his schooling.

- Charlie Chaplin once won third prize in a Charlie Chaplin lookalike contest.

- Christopher Columbus had blond hair.

- Dr Jekyll's first name is Henry.

ODDS AND ENDS

- Despite his great scientific and artistic achievement, Leonardo da Vinci was most proud of his ability to bend iron with his bare hands.

- Every time Beethoven sat down to write music, he poured ice water over his head.

- French astronomer Adrien Auzout once considered building a telescope that was 1,000 feet long in the 1600s. He thought the magnification would be so great he would see animals on the moon.

- Galileo became totally blind just before his death. This is probably because of his constant gazing at the sun through his telescope.

- Genghis Khan started out as a goatherd.

- Hans Christian Anderson, creater of fairy tales, was word-blind. He never learned to spell correctly, and his publishers always had errors.

- Harry Truman's middle name was just 'S'. It isn't short for anything. His parents could not decide between two different names beginning with S.

ODDS AND ENDS

- Hitler and Napolean both had only one testicle.

- Hitler was claustrophobic. The elevator leading to his Eagles' nest in the Austrian Alps was mirrored so it would appear larger and more open.

- Howard Hughes once made half a billion dollars in one day. In 1966, he received a bank draft for $546,549,171.00 in return for his 75 per cent holdings in TWA.

- Hrand Araklein, a Brink's car guard, was killed when $50,000 worth of quarters fell on and crushed him.

- In 1968, a convention of beggars in Dacca, India, passed a resolution demanding that the minimum amount of alms be fixed at 15 paisa (three cents).

- In 1976, a Los Angeles secretary named Jannene Swift officially married a 50-pound rock. The ceremony was witnessed by more than 20 people.

- John D Rockefeller was the first billionaire in the US.

- John Hancock was the only one of 50 signatories of the Declaration of Independence who actually signed it in July.

ODDS AND ENDS

- Jeremy Bentham, a British philosopher who died in 1832, left his entire estate to the London Hospital provided that his body preside over its board meetings. His skeleton was clothed and fitted with a wax mask of his face. It was present at the meeting for 92 years and can still be viewed there.

- John Lennon's first girlfriend was named Thelma Pickles.

- John Lennon's middle name was Winston.

- Leon Trotsky, the seminal Russian Communist, was assassinated in Mexico with an icepick.

- Leonardo da Vinci could write with one hand and draw with the other at the same time.

- Leonardo da Vinci invented the concept of the parachute, but his design was fatally flawed in that it did not allow air to pass through the top of the chute. Therefore, the chute would not fall straight, but would tilt to the side, lose its air and plummet.

- Leonardo da Vinci invented the scissors.

- Mr Mojo Risin is an anagram for Jim Morrison.

ODDS AND ENDS

- Mark Twain was born in 1835 when Halley's comet appeared. He died in 1910 when Halley's comet returned.

- Mozart is buried in an unmarked pauper's grave.

- Mozart wrote the nursery rhyme 'Twinkle Twinkle, Little Star' at the age of five.

- Napoleon conducted his battle plans in a sandbox.

- Napoleon had his boots worn by servants to break them in before he wore them.

- Napoleon Bonaparte was afraid of cats.

- Oliver Cromwell was hanged and decapitated two years after his death.

- Peter the Great executed his wife's lover and forced her to keep her lover's head in a jar of alcohol in her bedroom.

- Rita Moreno is the first and only entertainer to have received all four of America's top entertainment industry awards: the Oscar, the Emmy, the Tony and the Grammy.

ODDS AND ENDS

- Robert E. Lee wore size 4½ shoe.

- Robert E. Lee, of the Confederate Army, remains the only person, to date, to have graduated from the West Point military academy without a single demerit.

- Salvador Dali once arrived at an art exhibition in a limousine filled with turnips.

- Samuel Clemens, aka Mark Twain, smoked 40 cigars a day for the last years of his life.

- Sawney Beane, his wife, eight sons, six daughters and 32 grandchildren were a family of cannibals that lived in the caves near Galloway, Scotland in the early 17th century. Although the total number is not known, it is believed they claimed over 50 victims per year. The entire family was taken by an army detachment to Edinburgh and executed, apparently without trial.

- Sherlock Holmes never said, 'Elementary, my dear Watson'.

- Sister Boom-Boom was a transvestite nun who ran for mayor of San Francisco in 1982. He/she received over 20,000 votes.

ODDS AND ENDS

- Socrates committed suicide by drinking the poison hemlock.

- Socrates left no writings of his own.

- St Stephen is the patron saint of bricklayers.

- Stalin's left foot had webbed toes, and his left arm was noticably shorter.

- The first man to return safely from space was Yuri Gagarin.

- The world record for most children to one mother is 69 children.

- The world's youngest parents were eight and nine and lived in China in 1910.

- Thomas Edison, the inventor of the lightbulb, was afraid of the dark.

- The Red Baron's real name was Manfred Von Richtofen.

- Two sisters in the US, Susan and Deborah, weighed 205 and 124 pounds although they were only five and three years old respectively, in 1829.

ODDS AND ENDS

- Uri Geller, the professional psychic, was born in 1946. As to the origin of his alleged powers, Mr Geller maintains that they come from a distant planet of Hoova.

- Vincent Van Gogh comitted suicide while painting *Wheat Field with Crows*.

- Walt Disney's autograph bears no resemblance to the famous Disney logo.

- Warren Beatty and Shirley MacLaine are brother and sister.

- When Beethoven was a child, he made such a poor impression on his music teachers that he was pronounced hopeless as a composer.

- When young and impoverished, Pablo Picasso kept warm by burning his own paintings.

- Winston Churchill was born in a ladies' room during a dance.

- Worldwide there are more statues of Joan of Arc than of anyone else. France alone has about 40,000 of them.

11

PLACES, SPACE AND TRAVEL

PLACES, SPACE AND TRAVEL

- The English gold coin, the guinea, is named after the country in West Africa where the gold used to make it was originally mined.

- The Red Sea is so named after the algae that when dying turns the Red Sea's normally intense blue-green waters to red.

- In Verona, Italy, in which Shakespeare set his tragedy *Romeo and Juliet*, about a thousand letters arrive addressed to Juliet every Valentine's Day.

- In Iceland Domino's Pizza has reindeer sausage pie on its menu.

- In New Guinea more than 700 different native languages are spoken – which is a third of the world's known languages.

- Lake Nicaragua in Nicaragua has the only freshwater sharks in the world.

- If the ozone in the atmosphere were compressed to a pressure equal to that at the earth's surface, the layer would be only 3 mm thick.

PLACES, SPACE AND TRAVEL

- Thirty-eight per cent of North America is wilderness.

- The moon weighs 81,000 trillion tons.

- The only river to flow both north and south of the equator is the Congo River, which crosses the equator twice.

- Nullarbor Plain in south-west Australia gets its name from the Latin *nullus arbor* – 'no tree'.

- Ninety-nine per cent of the buildings in Reykjavik, the capital of Iceland, are heated by natural hot springs.

- The Bronx in New York City is named after the Bronx River. The Bronx River is named after the first European settler in the Bronx – the Scandanavian-born Jonas Bronck, who settled there in 1639.

- Monaco has the biggest per-capita ownership of Rolls Royce cars in the world. In the last survey, in the early 1990s, the figure was one for every 65.1 people.

- Desire Street, in New Orleans, runs directly alongside and parallel with Piety Street.

-------- **PLACES, SPACE AND TRAVEL** --------

- The London Underground station St John's Wood is the only station on the network that does not contain any of the letters of the word 'mackerel'.

- On the Pacific Gilbert and Ellis Islands, Britain's largest colonial territory, the highest point above sea level is 11 ft (3 m).

- The oldest surviving parliament is in Iceland. It first met in 930 when Viking chieftains met in the open air to argue their differences.

- Mount Cook in New Zealand is the largest mountain in Oceana, at 3,764 m.

- The driest place on earth is a series of valleys near Ross Island in Antarctica, where for at least the last two million years no rain has ever fallen.

- Devon is the only county in Great Britain to have two coasts.

- About one-tenth of the world's surface is permanently covered in ice.

———— PLACES, SPACE AND TRAVEL ————

- The smallest and shallowest ocean in the world is the Arctic Ocean.

- The Channel grows 300 mm each year.

- Woodward Avenue in Detroit, Michigan, carries the designation M-1 because it was the first paved road anywhere in the world.

- The word for 'name' in Japanese is '*na-ma-e*'. In Mongolian it is '*nameg*'.

- There is a Historical Museum of Spaghetti in Pontedassio, Italy.

- Jupiter is bigger than all the other planets in our solar system combined.

- The Niagara Falls have eaten their way seven miles (11 km) up stream since their formation 10,000 years ago. If erosion continues at this rate they will disappear into Lake Erie in 22,000 years.

- At latitude 60° south you can sail all the way around the world.

PLACES, SPACE AND TRAVEL

- The 1968 film *Krakatoa – East of Java* had a major fault. The volcano was in fact west of Java.

- Britain's shortest river is the Brun, which runs through Burnley in Lancashire.

- The highest wave ever recorded – towering a full ten-stories high – was 112 feet (34 m) high and seen in the North Pacific in 1933.

- The largest landlocked country in the world is Mongolia.

- Oxford Street, in London, is named after the Earl of Oxford and not because it, coincidentally, is the start of the main road from London to Oxford.

- In its lifetime the earth has been hit by at least one million meteors.

- Brazoria county in south-east Texas is the only county in the United States to have every kind of poisonous snake found in the United States and Canada.

- The earth's atmosphere is proportionately thinner than the skin of an apple.

PLACES, SPACE AND TRAVEL

- Lake Baikal, in southern Siberia, is the deepest lake in the world. It was formed 25 to 30 million years ago and is 1,743 m (5, 718 ft) deep.

- Ninety per cent of the world's ice is contained in the Antarctic ice sheet.

- The red supergiant star Betelgeuse has a diameter larger than that of the earth's orbit around the sun – 186 million miles (299,329,800 km).

- New Zealand is the only country that contains every type of climate in the world.

- When members of the nature-worshipping Southern Indian tribe Todas greet one another they thumb their noses instead of shaking hands.

- Australian $5, $10, $20, $50 and $100 notes are made of plastic.

- If you stand with your eyes about 6 ft (2 m) above the surface of the ocean the horizon will be about 3 miles (5 km) away.

PLACES, SPACE AND TRAVEL

- In 1929 Toronto, Ontario, in eastern Canada, became home to the biggest swimming pool in the world. The pool held 2,000 people and measured 300 by 75 ft (91 by 23 m). It is still in operation.

- When the University of Nebraska Cornhuskers play football at home the stadium becomes the third-largest city of the central US state.

- Singapore is the only country with only one train station.

- Uranus's axis of rotation is inclined 98° to the plain of its orbit – which means that it rotates on its side.

- The Angel of Independence in Mexico City was built by architect Antonio Rivas Mercado. The face of the angel is a portrait of his daughter.

- There are over 50,000 earthquakes a year around the world.

- If Brooklyn, New York, became independent of New York City it would become the third-largest city in the United States after the rest of New York and Los Angeles.

PLACES, SPACE AND TRAVEL

- Birmingham has more miles of canal than Venice.

- In Venice, Italy, all gondolas must be painted black unless they belong to a senior official.

- Australia is the only continent without an active volcano.

- Cyprus has a map on its flag.

- A hailstone containing a carp fell in Essen, Germany.

- Some Malaysians protect their babies from disease by bathing them in beer.

- At April 2000, Hong Kong had 392,000 faxlines – one of the highest rates of business fax use in the world.

- At Hancock Secondary School in Mississippi there is actually a McDonalds in the high school.

- At one point, the Circus Maximus in Rome could hold up to 250,000 people.

- Buckingham Palace has over 600 rooms.

PLACES, SPACE AND TRAVEL

- Built in 1697, the Frankford Avenue Bridge which crosses Pennypack Creek in Philadelphia is the oldest US bridge in continuous use.

- Coney Island, the amusement park, has had three of its rides designated as New York City historical landmarks.

- Construction on the Leaning Tower of Pisa began on 9 August, 1173.

- Disneyland opened in 1955.

- Due to precipitation, for a few weeks K2 is taller than Mt. Everest.

- Harvard uses Yale brand locks on their buildings; Yale uses Best brand.

- If a statue in the park of a person on a horse has both front legs in the air, the person died in battle; if the horse has one front leg in the air, the person died as a result of wounds received in battle; if the horse has all four legs on the ground, the person died of natural causes.

- If you divide the Great Pyramid's perimeter by two times its height, you get PI to the fifteenth digit.

—— PLACES, SPACE AND TRAVEL ——

- If you bring a raccoon's head to the Henniker, New Hampshire town hall, you are entitled to receive $10 from the town.

- In 1980, a Las Vegas hospital suspended workers for betting on when patients would die.

- In Paris, the McDonalds big 'M' is the only one in the world that is white, rather than yellow; it was thought that yellow was too tacky.

- In Washington DC no building can be built taller than the Washington Monument.

- It is forbidden for aircraft to fly over the Taj Mahal.

- Liberace Museum has a mirror-plated Rolls Royce, jewel-encrusted capes and the largest rhinestone in the world, weighing 59 pounds and measuring almost a foot in diameter.

- Los Angeles's full name is El Pueblo de Nuestra Senora la Reina de los Angeles de Porciuncula – and can be abbreviated to 6.3 per cent of its size: LA.

- Maine is the toothpick capital of the world.

PLACES, SPACE AND TRAVEL

- New York's Central Park is nearly twice the size of the entire country of Monaco.

- New York's Central Park opened in 1876.

- Printed on the book being held by the Statue of Liberty is 'July IV, MDCCLXXVI'.

- Since the 1930's the town of Corona, California has lost all 17 of the time capsules they originally buried.

- Some hotels in Las Vegas have gambling tables floating in their swimming pools.

- The Angel Falls in Venezuela are nearly 20 times taller than Niagara Falls.

- The blueprints for the Eiffel Tower covered more than 14,000 square feet of drafting paper.

- The clock at the National Bureau of Standards in Washington, DC will gain or lose only one second in 300 years because it uses cesium atoms.

- The Eiffel Tower was built for the 1889 World's Fair.

——— PLACES, SPACE AND TRAVEL ———

- The foundation of great European cathedrals go down as far as 40 or 50 feet.

- The Future's Museum in Sweden contains a scale model of the solar system. The sun is 105 metres in diameter and the planets range from 5mm to 6km from the 'sun'. This particular model also contains the nearest star Proxima Centauri, still to scale, situated in the Museum of Victoria ... in Australia.

- The Grand Canyon was not seen by a white man until after the Civil War. It was first entered on 29 May 1869 by the geologist John Wesley Powell.

- The Great Wall stretches for 4,160 miles across North China.

- The height of the Eiffel Tower varies as much as six inches depending on the temperature.

- The Hoover Dam was built to last 2,000 years. The concrete in it will not even be fully cured for another 500 years.

- The largest object that was ever found in the Los Angeles sewer system was a motorcycle.

---------------- **PLACES, SPACE AND TRAVEL** ----------------

- The main library at Indiana University sinks over an inch every year because when it was built engineers failed to take into account the weight of all the books that would occupy the building.

- The many sights that represent the Chinese city of Beijing were built by foreigners: the Forbidden City was built by the Mongols, the Temple of Heaven by the Manchurians.

- The name of the woman on the Statue of Liberty is Mother of Exiles.

- The names of the two stone lions in front of the New York Public Library are Patience and Fortitude. They were named by the then mayor Fiorello LaGuardia.

- The oldest university in the US is Harvard.

- The Pentagon in Washington, DC has five sides, five storeys and five acres in the middle.

- The San Diego Zoo in California has the largest collection of animals in the world.

- The Statue of Liberty's mouth is three feet wide.

—— PLACES, SPACE AND TRAVEL ——

- The University of Alaska stretches over four time zones.

- There are 47 czars buried within the Kremlin.

- There are 6,500 windows in the Empire State Building. There are more than 10 million bricks in the Empire State Building.

- There are no clocks in Las Vegas gambling casinos.

- There is a resort town in New Mexico called Truth or Consequences.

- There is a town in Texas called Ding Dong.

- There is an airport in Calcutta named Dum Dum Airport.

- There was once a town named '6' in West Virginia.

- There's a 'cemetery town' in California called Colma: its ratio of dead to living people is 750 to 1.

- There's a bathroom in Egypt where it is free to use the toilet, but you have to bring/buy your own toilet paper.

- Three Mile Island is only 2.5 miles long.

PLACES, SPACE AND TRAVEL

- The Sphinx at Giza in Egypt is 240 feet long and carved out of limestone. Built by Pharaoh Khafre to guard the way to his pyramid, it has a lion's body and the ruler's head.

RELIGION AND MYTHOLOGY

RELIGION AND MYTHOLOGY

- A bible published in England in 1632 missed out the word 'not' in the seventh commandment, making it 'Thou shalt commit adultery'. It became known as 'The Wicked Bible'.

- The only woman whose age is mentioned in the Bible is Sarah, who bore Abraham a child, Isaac, when she was 90. She was said to die at the age of 127.

- The most common name in the Bible is Zechariah. There are 33 of them.

- At 6 cubits and a span, Goliath's height was somewhere between nine feet three inches (3 m 8 cm) and eleven feet nine inches (3 m 23 cm). A cubit is the distance from the elbow to the end of the middle finger and can vary from 17 to 22 inches (43 to 56 cm). A span is the distance from the extended little fingertip to the end of the thumb and is approximately nine inches (23 cm).

- The Vikings had a god of snowshoes named Ull.

- Methuselah lived to be 969 years old, according to Genesis.

- When W C Fields was caught glancing through a bible he explained it with the words: 'Looking for loopholes'.

———RELIGION AND MYTHOLOGY———

● According to the Bible there are twelve pearly gates.

● In addition to the animals there were eight people on Noah's ark. Noah, his wife, his sons Shem, Ham and Japheth, and their wives.

● Delilah had to cut seven tresses of hair from Samson's head to render him powerless.

● Jesus is believed to have spoken Aramaic, the language then in use in the Arabian peninsular where he lived. A modern version of the language is still spoken in Syria.

● The world population at the time of the Crucifixion was about 200 million.

● Only one Englishman has become Pope in 2,000 years. He was Nicholas Breakspear, or Adrian IV, from 1154 to 1159.

● On 29 November 2000 Pope John Paul II was made an honorary Harlem Globetrotter.

● Xmas does not begin with the Roman letter X. It begins with the Greek letter '*chi*', which was used in medieval manuscripts as an abbreviation for the word 'Christ'. For example, 'Xus' equals 'Christus'.

───── RELIGION AND MYTHOLOGY─────

● Some biblical scholars believe that Aramaic did not contain a way of saying 'many' and used a term that has come down to us as '40'. This means that when the Bible refers to 40 days it actually means 'many days'.

● Nell Gwynne once quietened an angry Oxford crowd, who mistakenly believed she was Charles II's French Catholic mistress, by telling them: 'Pray, good people, be civil. I am the Protestant whore.'

● The shortest verse in the Bible is 'Jesus wept'.

● The only domestic animal not mentioned in the Bible is the cat.

● Prince Charles once threw the moderator of the Church of Scotland into a fountain at Balmoral.

● The American newspaper columnist H L Mencken wrote: 'Puritanism. The haunting fear that someone, somewhere, may be happy.'

● There are nine ranks of angels. From the highest to the lowest, they are Seraphims, Cherubims, Thrones, Dominions, Virtues, Powers, Principalities, Archangels and Angels.

————RELIGION AND MYTHOLOGY————

- Moses was 120 years old when he died.

- The holy cities of Islam are Mecca, Medina and Jerusalem.

- A church council in the twelfth century declared: 'A Christian man is bound to chastise his wife moderately.'

- When Lady Carina Fitzalan Howard was asked if her future husband, television interviewer David Frost, was religious, she replied: 'Yes, he thinks he's God almighty.'

- The film *The Ten Commandments*, in which Charlton Heston plays Moses, was the biggest cinema box-office earner of the 1950s.

- The savage Salem witch trials in the seventeenth century were all based on a single line in Exodus: 'Thou shalt not suffer a witch to live.'

- The Crystal Cathedral, founded by TV evangelist Robert Schuller, in Garden Grove, California, is longer than a football field and contains more than 10,000 panes of glass.

- Lord Hugh Cecil believed 'the two dangers which beset the Church of England are good music and bad preaching'.

-------- **RELIGION AND MYTHOLOGY**--------

- Brigham Young, the Mormon leader, married his 27th, and last, wife in 1868.

- According to Scottish novelist and politician John Buchan, 'An atheist is a man who has no invisible means of support.'

- A third of Taiwanese funeral processions include a stripper.

- Almost all the villains in the Bible have red hair.

- Christianity has over a billion followers. Islam is next in representation with half this number.

- In Turkey, the colour of mourning is violet. In most Muslim countries and in China it is white.

- It was only after 440 AD that 25 December was celebrated as the birth date of Jesus Christ.

- Kerimaki Church in Finland is the world's biggest church made of wood.

- Las Vegas has more chapels per capita than any other US city.

RELIGION AND MYTHOLOGY

- The last word in the Bible is Amen.

- The longest chapter in the Bible is Psalm 119.

- The practice of exchanging presents at Christmas originated with the Romans.

- The youngest pope was 11 years old.

- There are more than 1,700 references to gems and precious stones in the King James version of the Bible.

- Two-thirds of Portugal was owned by the Church in the early eighteenth century.

- Contrary to popular belief, there are almost no Buddhists in India, nor have there been for about a thousand years.

- Pope Adrian VI died after a fly got stuck in his throat as he was drinking from a water fountain.

- Hindu men once believed it to be unluckily to marry a third time. They could avoid misfortune by marrying a tree first. The tree (his third wife) was then burned, freeing him to marry again.

———RELIGION AND MYTHOLOGY———

- Husbands and wives in India who desire children whisper their wish to the ear of a sacred cow.

- According to ceremonial customs of Orthodox Judaism, it is officially sundown when you cannot tell the difference between a black thread and a red thread.

13

SPORT AND GAMES

SPORT AND GAMES

- A rodeo cowboy has to stay on the bull for only eight seconds in a bull-riding contest – but few make it.

- The discus throw is the only track-and-field event for which a world record has never been set in Olympic competition.

- The par for the world's longest golf hole – the 909-yard (831-m) seventh hole on Japan's Sano golf course – is 7.

- Heavyweight boxing champion Ken Norton was rejected for the role of Apollo Creed in the 1976 film *Rocky* because he made star Sylvester Stallone look too small.

- In the original Olympics, trainers were required to attend in the nude. This was to stop women sneaking into the competitions, from which they were banned. One woman had attended an event disguised as her son's trainer. Thereafter the nude ruling was brought in.

- In horse racing a walkover is when a horse is uncontested in a race and simply has to walk the course to win.

- Horse racing has a sex allowance. Mares are permitted to carry 3 to 5 lb (1 to 2 kg) less weight when running against males in a thoroughbred horse race.

SPORT AND GAMES

- The first man to run the four-minute mile, England's Roger Bannister, held the world-record title for only 46 days. Australian John Landy knocked 1.4 seconds off his time on 21 June 1954.

- The odds of getting four of a kind in a five-card deal in poker are 4,164 to 1.

- King James II of Scotland banned golf in 1457 because, he said, it distracted the men from archery practice needed for national defence.

- The French boxing federation officially banned fighters from kissing one another at the end of their bouts in 1924.

- A bad shot that turns out well in golf is known as a Volkswagen in golfing slang.

- In 1956 the Physical Culture and Sports Commission of communist China recognised the sport of hand-grenade throwing.

- The very first video game, introduced in 1972, was Pong.

--------------- **SPORT AND GAMES** ---------------

- America's last professional bare-knuckle boxing bout, in 1889, went to 75 rounds. The fight was between John L Sullivan and Jake Kilrain – Kilrain lost. The famous lawman Bat Masterson was the timekeeper.

- The odds against a professional golf player scoring a hole-in-one are 15,000 to 1 against.

- Catgut, used in stringing tennis racquets, comes from the intestines of sheep, horses and several other animals – but definitely not the cat. It is possible the word was shortened from the original 'cattlegut'.

- Fourteen-year-old Nadia Comaneci of Romania was the first ever to receive a perfect '10' in an Olympic gymnastic competition. That was in 1976.

- Horses race clockwise in England and anti-clockwise in the United States.

- The game of ninepins, taken to America by the Dutch in the seventeenth century, was changed to tenpins in the 1840s. Because of heavy gambling on the game New York and Connecticut banned ninepin bowling. But since the ban did not apply to bowling in general, a tenth pin was added to get around the law.

SPORT AND GAMES

- The word 'furlong' in horse racing – a distance of an eighth of a mile (201 m) – dates from the days when a race was a furrow long, the length of a ploughed field.

- There were no rounds when boxing was introduced at the 23rd ancient Olympiad in 776 BC. Contestants fought until one man either dropped or gave in. There were no breaks.

- In the ancient Olympic Games archers used tethered doves as targets.

- The heaviest heavyweight boxer to compete in a title fight was Italy's Primo Carnera, who weighed 19 stone 4 lb (270 lb or 122.5 kg) when he beat Tommy Loughran in 1934.

- The odds against hitting the jackpot on the average slot machine are 889 to 1.

- The French dice game known as 'Hazard' was introduced into the United States – in New Orleans – in 1813, by a Creole. Creoles, because of their French associations, were sometimes nicknamed Johnny Crapauds, the word 'crapaud' being French for toad or frog. At first it was referred to as Crapaud's game, but was later shortened to 'Craps'.

---------------- **SPORT AND GAMES** ----------------

- During a 100 m race a top sprinter makes contact with the ground only some 40 times.

- King George VI competed at Wimbledon in 1926 when he was Duke of York. The left-hander lost his first-round doubles match.

- All five sons of heavyweight boxing champion George Foreman are called George.

- The standard pitching distance in a game of horseshoes is 40 ft (12 m) for men and 30 ft (9 m) for women.

- The first driver to cover a mile in less than a minute in a petrol engine car was Barney Oldfield in 1903. He did a mile in 59.6 seconds driving a Ford 999.

- Professional boxing gloves weigh 8 oz (approx. 224 g).

- The first Indianapolis 500 motor race in 1911 was won at an average speed of 74.59 mph (120 kph).

- The game of billiards gave us the word 'debut'. It is derived from the French word '*débuter*' which means 'to lead off'.

—————— **SPORT AND GAMES** ——————

- The phrase 'turning point' comes from chariot racing. It was the place where a chariot driver turned at each end of the stadium.

- Anise is the scent on the artificial rabbit that is used in greyhound races.

- A forfeited game in baseball is recorded as a 9–0 score. In American football it is recorded as a 1–0 score.

- Australian Rules football was originally designed to give cricketers something to play during the off season.

- Canada is the only country not to win a gold medal in the summer Olympic games while hosting the event.

- Dartboards are made out of horse hairs.

- Four men in the history of boxing have been knocked out in the first 11 seconds of the first round.

- In 1936, American track star Jesse Owens beat a racehorse over a 100-yard course. The horse was given a head start.

--------- **SPORT AND GAMES** ---------

- In the four professional major North American sports (baseball, basketball, football and hockey) there are only seven teams whose nicknames do not end with an S. These teams are the Miami Heat, the Utah Jazz, the Orlando Magic, the Boston Red Sox, the Chicago White Sox, the Colorado Avalanche, the Tampa Bay Lightning, and the Minnesota Wild.

- In the United States, more Frisbee discs are sold each year than baseballs, basketballs, and footballs combined.

- Kite flying is a professional sport in Thailand.

- Morihei Ueshiba, founder of Aikido, once pinned a Sumo wrestler using only a single finger.

- Nearly all Sumo wrestlers have flat feet and big bottoms.

- Only two countries have participated in every modern Olympic Games, Greece and Australia.

- Pole vault poles used to be stiff. Now they bend which allows the vaulter to go much higher.

- Sprinters on track teams started taking a crouching start in 1908.

———— SPORT AND GAMES ————

- Ten events make up the decathlon.

- The 1912, Greco-Roman wrestling match in Stockholm between Finn Alfred Asikainen and Russian Martin Klein lasted more than 11 hours.

- The expression 'getting someone's goat' is based on the custom of keeping a goat in the stable with a racehorse as the horse's companion. The goat becomes a settling influence on the thoroughbred. If you owned a competing horse and were not above some dirty business, you could steal your rival's goat (seriously, it's been done) to upset the other horse and make it run a poor race. From goats and horses it was linguistically extended to people: in order to upset someone, get their goat.

- The national sport of Japan is sumo wrestling.

- The only bone not broken so far during any ski accident is one located in the inner ear.

- There are at least two sports in which the team has to move backwards to win – tug of war and rowing.

- Tokyo has the world's biggest bowling alley.

---------------- **SPORT AND GAMES** ----------------

- Tug of war was an Olympic event between 1900 and 1920.

- A baseball has exactly 108 stitches.

- Bank robber John Dillinger played professional baseball.

- Baseball's home plate is 17 inches wide.

- Before 1859, baseball umpires used to sit on rocking chairs behind the home plate.

- Basketball was invented by Canadian James Naismith in 1891.

- Michael Jordan makes more money from Nike annually than all of the Nike factory workers in Malaysia combined.

- Michael Jordan shaves his head on Tuesdays and Fridays.

- The theme song of the Harlem Globetrotters is 'Sweet Georgia Brown'.

- The bowling ball was invented in 1862.

—————— SPORT AND GAMES ——————

- Boxing is considered the easiest sport for gamblers to fix.

- Boxing rings are called rings because they used to be round.

- In 1985, Mike Tyson started boxing professionally at age 18.

- The most popular sport as a topic for a film is boxing.

- In the movie *Toy Story*, the carpet design in Sid's hallway is the same as the carpet design in *The Shining*.

- An American football has four seams.

- Green Bay Packers backup quarterback Matt Hasselbeck has been struck by lightning twice in his life.

- It takes 3,000 cows to supply the NFL with enough leather for a year's supply of footballs.

- OJ Simpson had a severe case of rickets and wore leg braces when he was a child.

- The Super Bowl is broadcast in 182 countries. That is more than 88 per cent of the countries in the world.

SPORT AND GAMES

- When the University of Nebraska Cornhuskers play American football at home, the stadium becomes the state's third largest city.

- Before 1850, golf balls were made of leather and stuffed with feathers.

- Golfing great Ben Hogan's famous reply when asked how to improve one's game was: 'Hit the ball closer to the hole'.

- In the US, there are more then 10,000 golf courses.

- Many Japanese golfers carry hole-in-one insurance, because it is traditional in Japan to share one's good luck by sending gifts to all your friends when you get an ace. The price for what the Japanese term 'an albatross' can often reach $10,000.

- Someone constructs 12 new golf holes every day.

- The Tom Thumb golf course was the first miniature golf course in the United States. It was built it 1929 in Chattanooga, Tennessee by John Garnet Carter.

SPORT AND GAMES

- The only person ever to play golf on the moon was Alan Shepard. They never found the ball.

- The world's biggest bunker is Hell's Half Acre on the 535m 585yd seventh hole of the Pine Valley course, Clementon, NJ, built in 1912 and generally regarded as the world's most trying course.

- There are three golf balls sitting on the moon.

- There are 336 dimples on a regulation golf ball.

- A hockey puck is one inch thick.

- Canada imports about 850 Russian made hockey sticks on an average day.

- Professional hockey players skate at average speeds of 20-25mph.

- Bulgaria was the only football team in the 1994 World Cup in which all the players, last names ended with the letters OV.

- Football is played in more countries than any other sport.

SPORT AND GAMES

- Football legend Pele's real name is Edson Arantes do Nascimento.

- The group Simply Red is named after its love for the football team, Manchester United who have a red home strip.

- A top freestyle swimmer achieves a speed of only four miles per hour. Fish in contrast, have been clocked at 68mph.

14

FOOD

—————————— FOOD ——————————

- Tabasco sauce is made by fermenting vinegar with hot peppers in a French oak barrel, which has three inches of salt on top and is aged for three years until all the salt is defused through the barrel.

- After a coffee seed is planted it takes five years before the resulting plant can produce consumable fruit.

- Tic-Tacs contain carnauba wax – the same ingredient found in many car polishes.

- After the Popeye cartoon started in 1931 spinach consumption in the United States went up by 33%.

- The oldest recipe in existence is a recipe for beer.

- The ancient Romans often paid their taxes in honey.

- More cat food is bought in Britain each year than can be eaten by the number of cats in the country.

- A can of Spam is opened every four seconds.

- Almonds are members of the peach family.

FOOD

● Butter was the first food product allowed to have artificial colouring by law. It is totally white in its natural state.

● You can make a glass of apple cider with only three apples.

● Cream does not weigh as much as milk.

● Cranberries are sorted for ripeness by bouncing them. A ripe cranberry can be dribbled like a basketball.

● Germany has a beer ice cream in Popsicle form. Its alcohol content is lower than that of normal beer.

● More people are allergic to cow's milk than to any other food.

● Manufacturers of Old Grandad whisky produced their product throughout Prohibition by marking the bottles 'for medicinal purposes'.

● You cannot taste food unless it is mixed with saliva. This is true for all foods.

● French fries were invented in Belgium.

FOOD

- The nutmeg tree produces two spices. Nutmeg is from the nut kernel itself and mace comes from the kernel's lacy covering.

- In 1867 Napoleon III commanded chemists to produce a special kind of food for the army and navy. It was margarine.

- The Muppet Miss Piggy said: 'Never eat more than you can lift.'

- Bombay duck is dry, salted fish.

- It takes 75,000 crocus flowers to produce 1 lb (0.5 kg) of saffron – which is why it is the most expensive spice in the world.

- The herring is the most widely eaten fish in the world.

- Dr Miles's compound extract of tomato – an early ketchup – was sold as a medicine in the nineteenth century.

- Queen Victoria mixed her claret with whisky. The resulting brew was her favourite alcoholic drink.

---------------------------------- **FOOD** ----------------------------------

- Black-eyed peas are beans.

- Pepper is the top-selling spice in the world. The second is mustard.

- In order for decaffeinated coffee to be so labelled it must have 97% of its caffeine removed, under American federal regulations.

- Guests to multi-millionaire Alfred de Rothschild's mansion, in Buckinghamshire, England, who asked for milk in their tea were offered a choice between 'Hereford, Jersey or Shorthorn'!

- The first name of blind cellar monk Dom Perignon, who discovered champagne, was Pierre.

- The father of the Gimlet cocktail was Sir T O Gimlette, a British naval surgeon who insisted his fellow officers drink gin and lime juice as he believed it to be healthier than drinking neat gin.

- Ancient Egyptians would place their right hands on an onion when swearing on oath. Its round shape symbolised eternity.

---------------------- **FOOD** ----------------------

- The largest fruit crop on earth is grapes – followed by bananas.

- New Orleans, US, consumes more ketchup per capita than any other place on earth.

- Eighty-seven per cent of fully fat milk is water.

- 400 quarter-pounders can be made out of one cow.

- Seven per cent of Americans eat McDonalds each day.

- A can of Diet Coke will float in water while a can of regular Coke sinks.

- A company in Taiwan makes dinnerware out of wheat, so you can eat your plate.

- A full seven per cent of the entire Irish barley crop goes to the production of Guinness beer.

- A hard-boiled egg will spin. An uncooked or soft-boiled egg will not.

- A Saudi Arabian women can get a divorce if her husband doesn't give her coffee.

FOOD

- Almonds are the oldest, most widely cultivated and extensively used nuts in the world.

- Almost 425,000 hotdogs and buns, 160,000 hamburgers and cheeseburgers were served at Woodstock '99.

- As much as 50 gallons of Maple Sap are used to make a single gallon of Maple Sugar.

- Astronauts are not allowed to eat beans before they go into space because passing wind in a spacesuit damages them.

- Beer foam will go down if you lick your finger then stick it in the beer.

- Blueberry Jelly Bellies were created especially for Ronald Reagan.

- Bubble gum contains rubber.

- California's Frank Epperson invented the Popsicle in 1905 when he was 11 years old.

- Chefs started using onions 5,000 years ago to spice up their cooking.

----------------- FOOD -----------------

- Chewing gum while peeling onions will keep you from crying.

- China produces 278,564,356,980 eggs per year.

- China's Beijing Duck Restaurant can seat 9,000 people at one time.

- Coca-Cola was first served in Atlanta, USA (Jacob's Pharmacy) in 1886 for only 5 cents a glass. The formula for Coca-Cola was created by pharmacist John Pemberton.

- Coca-Cola was originally green.

- Coffee does not help sober up a drunk person. In many cases it may actually increase the adverse effects of alcohol.

- Coffee is the world's most popular stimulant.

- Coke is used to clean up blood spills on highways.

- Cranberry jelly is the only jelly flavour that comes from the real fruit, not artificial flavouring.

---------------- **FOOD** ----------------

- Diet Coke was only invented in 1983.

- Doughnuts originated in Holland.

- Dry cereal for breakfast was invented by John Henry Kellogg at the turn of the century.

- Dunkin' Donuts serves about 112,500 doughnuts each day.

- During your lifetime you will eat 60,000 pounds of food, the weight of six elephants.

- Each year, Americans spend more on cat food than on baby food.

- Fanta Orange is the third largest selling soft drink in the world.

- Five jelly flavours that flopped: celery, coffee, cola, apple and chocolate.

- Fortune cookies were actually invented in America, in 1918, by Charles Jung.

FOOD

- France has the highest per capita consumption of cheese.

- Honey is used as a centre for golf balls and in antifreeze mixtures.

- If China imported just 10 per cent of its rice needs the price on the world market would increase by 80 per cent.

- If you put a raisin in a glass of champagne, it will keep floating to the top and sinking to the bottom.

- In 1865 opium was grown in the state of Virginia and a product was distilled from it that yielded four per cent morphine. In 1867 it was grown in Tennessee; six years later it was cultivated in Kentucky. During these years opium, marijuana and cocaine could be purchased legally over the counter from any chemist.

- In 1983, a Japanese artist made a copy of the *Mona Lisa* completely out of toast.

- In cooking, six drops make a dash.

- It takes more than 500 peanuts to make one 12-ounce jar of peanut butter.

FOOD

- It is estimated that Americans will consume 10 million tons of turkey on Thanksgiving Day. Due to turkey's high sulphur content, Americans will also produce enough gas to fly a fleet of 75 Hindenburghs from LA to New York in 24 hours.

- Japan is the largest exporter of frogs' legs.

- Ketchup originated in China.

- Laws forbidding the sale of sodas on Sunday prompted William Garwood to invent the ice cream sundae in Evanston, IL, in 1875.

- M&M's stands for the last names of Forrest Mars Sr., the sweet maker, and his associate Bruce Murrie.

- M&M's were developed so soldiers could eat the sweets without getting their fingers sticky.

- Mexican jumping beans jump because of a moth larva inside the bean.

- More than half of the different types of cheese in the world come from France.

--------------------------------- **FOOD** ---------------------------------

- Nicotine was introduced by Jean Nicot (French Ambassador to Portugal) in France in 1560.

- No two cornflakes look the same.

- Britain's most popular snack food is potato crisps.

- Nutmeg is extremely poisonous if injected intravenously.

- One of the ingredients in some ice cream is seaweed.

- Only five per cent of salt produced ends up on the dinner table. The rest is used for packing meat, building roads, feeding livestock, tanning leather and manufacturing glass, soap, ash and washing compounds.

- The only food that does not spoil is honey.

- Peanuts are one of the ingredients of dynamite.

- Pepsi is commonly used by wooden boat owners to clean mould from decks. You can spill it on for about 30 seconds, but it needs rinsing to make sure it does not erode your decks completely.

- Pepsi originally contained pepsin, therefore the name.

———————— **FOOD** ————————

- People spend a lot more money on groceries when they shop on a hungry stomach.

- Potato crisps were invented in Louisiana in 1853.

- Potatoes were first imported by Europe in the 1500s on Spanish ships returning from Peru.

- Pound for pound, hamburgers cost more than new cars.

- Rice is grown on more than 10 per cent of the earth's farmable surface.

- Rice is the main food for half of the people of the world.

- Rice is thrown at weddings as a symbol of fertility.

- Salt is one of the few spices that is all taste and no smell.

- Salt is the only rock humans can eat.

- Since 1978, at least 37 people have died as a result of shaking vending machines, in an attempt to get free merchandise. More than 100 have been injured.

---------------------------------- **FOOD** ----------------------------------

- Small flat icebergs have been fitted with sails and piloted more than 2,400 miles from the Antarctic to Valparaiso, Chile, and to Cakkaiub, Peru.

- Some people drink the urine of pregnant women to build up their immune system.

- Table salt is the only commodity that hasn't risen dramatically in price in the last 150 years.

- The biggest selling restaurant food is french fries.

- The Bloody Mary is known as the 'Queen of Drinks'. and was invented in Harry's Bar, Paris in the 1930s.

- The citrus soda 7-UP was created in 1929; 7 was selected because the original containers were 7 ounces. UP indicated the direction of the bubbles.

- The colour of a chilli is no indication of its spiciness, but size usually is – the smaller the pepper, the hotter it is.

- The dark meat on a roast turkey has more calories than the white meat.

FOOD

- The first man to distill bourbon whiskey was a Baptist preacher in 1789.

- The glue on Israeli postage stamps is certified kosher.

- The heat of peppers is rated on the Scoville scale.

- The hottest chile in the world is the habanero.

- The largest apple pie ever baked was 40 by 23 feet.

- The largest hamburger in the world weighed in at 5,520 pounds.

- The largest ketchup bottle is a 170 feet (52m) water tower.

- The liquid inside young coconuts can be used as a substitute for blood plasma in an emergency.

- The number 57 on a Heinz ketchup bottle represents the number of varieties of pickle the company once had.

- The top layer of a wedding cake, known as the groom's cake, is usually a fruit cake so it will last until the couple's first anniversary, when they will eat it.

---------------------------------- **FOOD** ----------------------------------

- The wheat that produces a one-pound loaf of bread requires two tons of water to grow.

- The world's number one producer and consumer of fresh pork is China.

- There are 2 million different combinations of sandwiches that can be created from a SUBWAY menu.

- There are more than 100 chemicals in one cup of coffee.

- There are only two people in the world that know the secret recipe for Coca-Cola.

- There is cyanide in apple pips.

- Virginia Woolfe wrote all her books standing up.

- When a coffee seed is planted, it takes five years to yield consumable fruit.

- When honey is swallowed, it enters the blood stream within a period of 20 minutes.

FOOD

- Widows of a recently deceased king among the Baganda people of Uganda, have the honour of drinking the beer in which the king's entrails have been cleaned.

- Wine will spoil if exposed to light, hence tinted bottles.

- You should not eat a crayfish with a straight tail. It was dead before it was cooked.

- Bananas do not grow on trees, but on rhizomes.

- Fresh apples float because 25 per cent of their volume is air.

- Grapes explode when you put them in the microwave.

- Lemons contain more sugar than strawberries.

- Pineapples do not ripen after they have been picked.

- Seeds are missing from a navel orange.

- The avocado has the most calories of any fruit.

- Tomatoes and cucumbers are fruits.

FOOD

- In a typical restaurant, customers receive 27 pence worth of food for each pound they spend.

- 90 per cent of vitamin C in brussels sprouts will be lost in cooking.

- Ray Kroc bought McDonalds for $2.7 million in 1961 from the McDonald brothers.

- Ninety-six per cent of a cucumber is water.

- Apples, not caffeine, are more efficient for waking you up in the morning.

- Eating raw onions is good for unblocking a stuffed nose.

- Onions get their distinctive smell by soaking up sulphur from the soil.

- The oldest known vegetable is the pea.

- 'Tomatina' is the legendary Spanish tomato-throwing festival.

- Turnips turn green when sunburned.

———— FOOD ————

- You use more calories eating celery than there are in celery itself.

- Drinking water after eating reduces the acid in your mouth by 61 per cent.

- H_2O expands as it freezes and contracts as it melts, displacing the exact same amount of fluid in either state. So if the northern ice cap did melt, it would cause absolutely no rise in the level of the ocean.

- Hot water is heavier than cold.

- In the typical Canadian home, 45 per cent of water is used for the toilet, 28 per cent is used for bathing and personal matters, 23 per cent is used for laundry or dishes and four per cent is used for cooking or drinking purposes.

- Less than two per cent of the water on earth is fresh.

- There is a tea in China called white tea which is simply boiled water.

15

SEX

---------------------- SEX ----------------------

- Elvis Presley called his penis 'Little Elvis.'

- A recent survey revealed that 25% of Swedish women had had sex with more than 50 men.

- Americans spend more money each year at strip clubs than at all the theatres and classical concert halls in the country combined.

- The Ramses condom is named after the great pharaoh Ramses II, who fathered more than 160 children!

- In ancient Rome men found guilty of rape had their testicles crushed between two stones as a punishment.

- The word 'pornography' is from the Greek *pornographus*, meaning 'writing about prostitutes'.

- Married women are physically and mentally less healthy than single women.

- Nudity in public was considered perfectly acceptable in ancient Greece, but it was declared indecent if a man revealed an erection.

- The average person spends two weeks of their life kissing.

SEX

- Prostitutes revealed in a recent survey that the sexual act they are most often asked to perform is fellatio.

- The sperm count of American men is down 30% on 30 years ago.

- Residents of the island of Lesbos are Lesbosians, not Lesbians. Lesbians are so called because the Greek poet Sappho was from Lesbos. Many of her poems expressed her love for women, giving rise to her association with female homosexuality.

- According to a Caribbean cruise line 58% of the passengers are unable to wait more than ten hours before making love. A lifeboat is the fourth most popular place on a ship to have sex. The whirlpool bath is ranked the first.

- The average sexually active woman has sex 83 times a year.

- A candle is the artificial device most frequently used by women during masturbation, according to a recent American survey.

- In ancient Greece and Rome dildos were made out of animal horn, ivory, gold, silver – or even glass.

SEX

- Placing a red light outside a brothel to advertise its wares was first introduced in 1234 in Avignon, France.

- Forty-six per cent of women say a good night's sleep is better than sex.

- Eleven per cent of women and 5% of men claim never to have masturbated.

- Menstrual cramps have been known, in rare cases, to induce orgasm.

- Seventy-one per cent of women between the ages of eighteen and twenty are at ease being seen nude by their lover; 51% of men are at ease being seen nude by their girlfriend.

- Most American women say they would rather receive chocolate than flowers on St Valentine's Day.

- Humans spend two years of their lives making love.

- Only 31% of men admit to looking at other woman when in the company of their spouse or girlfriend. Their partners say this figure is actually 64%.

SEX

- On average it takes two tablespoons of blood to make a man's penis erect.

- Seventy per cent of Swedish women claim to have participated in a threesome.

- Every year more than 11,000 Americans hurt themselves trying out bizarre sexual positions.

- Sex burns off 360 calories an hour.

- America's first manufactured condoms appeared in 1870 and were made of vulcanised rubber. They were thick, insensitive and intended to be reused.

- A winged penis was the city symbol of Pompeii, the ancient Roman resort town destroyed by the eruption of Mount Vesuvius.

- Homosexuality was still on the American Psychiatric Association's list of mental illnesses until 1973.

- The average penguin has only one orgasm a year.

- Less than 30% of parents say they can openly discuss sex with their children.

--------------------------- SEX ---------------------------

- A real orgasm is said to burn 112 calories. A fake orgasm is said to burn off 315 calories.

- The heart beats faster during a brisk walk or a good argument than it does during sexual intercourse.

- Four popes died while participating in sexual acts.

16

STATISTICS

STATISTICS

- Sixty-seven per cent of dog owners buy holiday gifts for their pet.

- Sixty per cent of British women believe their legs to be about average.

- Thirty per cent of British women think their legs are poor.

- One per cent of British women think their legs are perfect.

- Thirty-nine per cent of women who think their legs are fat still wear short skirts.

- The dead outnumber the living on earth by about 25 to 1.

- The Battle of Waterloo lasted nine and a half hours.

- The odds of being in a plane crash are 1 in 750,000.

- Twelve per cent of the British population are left-handed.

- Forty-four per cent of all adults are estimated to go on a diet at least once a year.

STATISTICS

- Only 55% of Americans know that the sun is a star.

- If you gave every human on earth their own piece of land then, counting uninhabitable areas, each one would get 100 square feet.

- The average person laughs thirteen times a day.

- The average person over 50 will have spent a year looking for lost or mislaid items.

- Eighty-three per cent of people hit by lightning are men.

- Ten per cent of men do not care what their partners' legs look like.

- Ninety per cent of bird species are monogamous.

- Fifty per cent of Western women say they would marry the same man again; 80% of men say they would marry the same woman again.

- Fifty-eight per cent of men say they are happier after their divorce or separation.

- There is a lawsuit every 30 seconds in the United States.

STATISTICS

- Eighty-five per cent of women say they are happier after their divorce or separation.

- The odds of being hit by space debris are one in five billion.

- Right-handed people live, on average, nine years longer than left-handed people.

- On average, each year 55,700 people are injured by jewellery.

- Driving at 55 mph (89 kph) instead of 65 mph (105 kph) increases your car mileage by about 15%.

- Six per cent of American men say they proposed to their wives on the phone.

- Sixty-eight per cent of teenage girls would choose their stomach if they were allowed to change one part of their body.

- Twenty-two per cent of men leave their Christmas shopping until the last two days before Christmas Day. Only 9% of women do the same.

STATISTICS

- The average human produces 50,000 pints (28,400 litres) of spit in a lifetime – the equivalent of two small swimming pools.

- Forty per cent of Scottish women have legs that are different lengths.

- The average person in America spends eight years of their lives watching television.

- Twelve per cent of people start their Christmas shopping with the January sales.

- Eighty-five per cent of men do not use the front opening of their underpants when they urinate.

- Women shoplift more often than men; the statistics are four to one.

- The longest kiss on record lasted 130 hours and two minutes.

- The world record for carrying a milk bottle on your head is 24 miles.

STATISTICS

- 0.3 per cent of all road accidents in Canada involve a moose.

- Thirteen people a year are killed by vending machines falling on them.

- Four per cent of the US population are vegetarians.

- Forty per cent of women have hurled footwear at a man.

- Fifty per cent of teenage boys say that they would rather be rich than smart.

- Fifty-six per cent of the video game market is adults.

- Seven per cent of Americans think Elvis is alive.

- Eighty-two per cent of the world's population believe in an after life.

- Nine per cent of Americans have reported having been in the presence of a ghost.

- Ninety per cent of women who walk into a department store immediately turn to the right.

STATISTICS

- About one out of every 70 people who pick their nose actually eat their bogies.

- About five per cent of Americans claim to have talked to the devil personally.

- About six per cent of murdered American men are killed by either their wife or girlfriend ... or wife who caught them with their girlfriend.

- About 200 babies are born worldwide every minute.

- Approximately 97.35618329 per cent of all statistics are made up.

- Assuming Rudolph was in front, there are 40,320 ways to rearrange the other eight reindeer.

- Did you know that you're more likely to be killed by a champagne cork than a poisonous spider?

- Experienced waitresses say that married men tip better than unmarried men.

- In Calcutta, 79 per cent of the population live in one-room houses.

STATISTICS

- In Japan, 20 per cent of all publications sold are comic books.

- In the next seven days, 800 Americans will be injured by their jewellery.

- It is estimated that at any one time, 0.7 per cent of the world's population are drunk.

- It would take more than 150 years to drive a car to the sun.

- More people are killed by donkeys annually than are killed in plane crashes.

- More than 10 per cent of all the salt produced annually in the world is used to de-ice American roads.

- Nobody yet has explained satisfactorily why couples who marry in January, February and March tend to have the highest divorce rates.

- Odds of being killed by a dog are one in 700,000.

- Odds of being killed by a tornado are one in two million.

STATISTICS

- Odds of being killed by falling out of bed are one in two million.

- Odds of being killed in a car crash are one in 5,000.

- Odds of dying in the bathtub are one in one million.

- Of the 266 men who have been pope, 33 have died violently.

- Only 55 per cent of Americans know that the sun is a star.

- Over 50 per cent of Americans believe in the devil.

- Statistically the safest age of life is 10 years old.

- The average adult spends about 12 minutes in the shower.

- The average four-year-old child asks over 400 questions a day.

- The average person speaks about 31,500 words per day.

——————————— STATISTICS ———————————

- The average person spends about two years on the phone in a lifetime.

- The average person will spend two weeks over their lifetime waiting for the traffic lights to change.

- The murder rate in the United States is 200 times greater than in Japan. In Japan no private citizen can buy a handgun legally.

- Thirty-five per cent of the people who use personal ads for dating are already married.

- Twelve babies will be given to the wrong parents each day.

- You are more likely to get attacked by a cow than a shark.

17

LAST WORDS

LAST WORDS

- 'This is no time to be making new enemies.'

    Voltaire, in reply to the Bishop of Paris when asked on his deathbed to renounce the devil and turn to God.

- 'The earth is suffocating. Swear to make them cut me open, so I won't be buried alive.'

    Frederic Chopin

- 'I've had eighteen straight whiskies – I think that's a record. After 39 years this is all I've done.'

    Dylan Thomas

- 'Tell me, Gene, is it true you're the illegitimate son of Buffalo Bill Cody?'

    Actor John Barrymore, speaking to a deathbed friend

- 'If I say goodnight to you now, will you promise that I won't wake up again?'

    Film producer Alexander Korda

- 'I think I could eat one of Bellamy's veal pies.'

    Prime Minister Pitt the Younger

- 'Dammit. Put them back on. This is funny.'

    Gunfighter 'Doc' Holliday, after his boots were removed

LAST WORDS

● 'You can do that more easily to my dead body.
Come, be quick!'

> *Louis Philippe, Duke of Orleans, speaking
> to the executioner removing his boots*

● 'The bullet hasn't been made that can kill me.'

> *Gangster 'Legs' Diamond*

● 'Get my "swan" costume ready.'

> *Russian ballerina Anna Pavlova*

● 'Drink to me.'

> *Pablo Picasso*

● 'I can't sleep.'

> *Peter Pan author James Barrie*

● 'It would really be more than the English could stand if
another century began and I were still alive. I am dying
as I have lived – beyond my means.'

> *Oscar Wilde*

● 'Be natural, my children. For the writer that is natural
has fulfilled all the rules of art.'

> *Charles Dickens*

LAST WORDS

- 'Take away those pillows – I shall need them no more.'

  Lewis Carroll (Charles Lutwidge Dodgson)

- 'What is the noise?'

  Daughter: 'It's the people outside.'

  'What are they doing?'

  Daughter: 'They've come to say "Goodbye".'

  'Why? Where are they going?'

  Dictator Generalissimo Franco

- 'Nothing but death.'

  Jane Austen, when asked if she wanted anything

- 'If I feel in good form I shall take the difficult way up. If I do not, I shall take the easy way up. I shall join you in an hour.'

  King Alfred I of Belgium, killed mountain climbing

- 'Prithee, let me feel the axe. I fear it is not sharp enough. Do not hack me as you did my Lord Russell.'

  James, Duke of Monmouth, beheaded

- 'Oh God, here I go!'

  Heavyweight boxer Max Baer

——— LAST WORDS ———

- 'Can this last long?'

  King William III

- 'In the name of modesty, cover my bosom.'

  Elizabeth, sister of King Louis XVI, guillotined

- 'I am always angry when I'm dying.'

  Clifford Mortimer, barrister father of John

- 'Goodnight, my darlings, I'll see you tomorrow.'

  Noel Coward

- 'I've never felt better.'

  Actor Douglas Fairbanks Sr

- 'Do you know where the apothecary lives? Then send and let him know that I would like to see him. I don't feel quite well and I will lie still until he comes.'

  Duke of Wellington

- 'Sister, you're trying to keep me alive as an old curiosity. But I'm done. I am finished. I'm going to die.'

  George Bernard Shaw

- 'Well I've played everything but a harp.'

  Lionel Barrymore

LAST WORDS

• 'I desire to go to hell and not to heaven. In the former place I will enjoy the company of popes, kings and princes, while in the latter only beggars, monks and apostles.'

Niccolò Machiavelli

• 'That was the best ice-cream soda I ever tasted.'

US comedian Lou Costello

• 'See that Yul (Brynner) gets star billing. He has earned it.'

Gertrude Lawrence, star of the film The King and I

• 'If you would send for a doctor I will see him now.'

Emily Brontë

• 'Now I want to go home. Don't weep. What I have done is best for all of us. No use. I shall never get rid of this depression.'

Vincent van Gogh

• 'I guess you were right, Wyatt. I can't see a damn thing.'

Police officer Morgan Earp, speaking to his brother,
Wyatt, who denied afterlife existed

• 'I should never have switched from Scotch to Martinis.'

Humphrey Bogart

─────────── **LAST WORDS** ───────────

● 'This is it. I'm going. I'm going.'
Al Jolson, Russian-born American singer,
film actor and comedian

● 'I'm going. Perhaps it is for the best.'
US President John Tyler

● 'This is my final word. It is time for me to become an apprentice once more. I have not settled in which direction. But somewhere. Sometime. Soon.'
Lord Beaverbrook, British Conservative politician
and newspaper proprietor

● 'There is no one in the kingdom that will make me his master. My time has come to die.'
Confucius

● 'On the whole, I would rather be in Philadelphia.'
W C Fields

● 'I do not know which is more difficult in a Christian life – to live well or to die well.'
Daniel Defoe

LAST WORDS

- 'May I please have a cigar?'

  John Ford, film director

- 'I think it's time for morphine.'

  D H Lawrence

- 'Please put out the light.'

  US President Theodore Roosevelt

- 'The executioner is, I believe, an expert and my neck is very slender. Oh God, have pity on my soul.'

  Anne Boleyn

- 'I can't feel anything in my right leg. I can't feel anything in my left leg. Doctor, are my eyes open? I can't see.'

  'Manolete', matador

- 'I always was beautiful.'

  Pauline Bonaparte, Napoleon's sister

- 'What is the scaffold? A short-cut to heaven.'

  Charles Peace, hanged killer

- 'I have offended God and mankind because my work did not reach the quality it should have.'

  Leonardo da Vinci

——— LAST WORDS ———

- 'Excuse my dust.'

  Dorothy Parker, wit

- 'Now I know that I must be very ill, as you have been sent for.'

  Henry Longfellow, poet

- 'My fun days are over.'

  James Dean

- 'Remember me to my friends. Tell them I'm a hell of a mess.'

  H L Mencken, journalist

- 'What matter how the head lie, so the heart be right? 'Tis a sharp remedy, but a sure one for all ills.'

  Sir Walter Raleigh, when told his head lay the wrong way for beheading

- 'A king should die standing up.'

  Louis XVIII of France, trying to rise

- 'That was a great game of golf.'

  Bing Crosby

—————— **LAST WORDS** ——————

- 'Go away. I'm all right.'

  H G Wells

- 'God bless. Goddamn!'

  James Thurber, cartoonist

- 'Better not. She would only ask me to take a
  message to Albert.'

  *Prime Minister Benjamin Disraeli, asked if he wished to see
  Queen Victoria at his deathbed*

- 'If this is dying, then I don't think much of it.'

  Lytton Strachey, English author

18

END QUOTES

---------- **END QUOTES** ----------

● 'Death is the most convenient time to tax rich people.'
Prime Minister David Lloyd George

● 'Once you're dead, you're made for life.'
Jimi Hendrix

● 'Either he's dead or my watch has stopped.'
Groucho Marx

● 'He makes a very nice corpse, and becomes his coffin prodigiously.'
Oliver Goldsmith, Irish novelist, poet,
essayist and dramatist

● 'It's not that I'm afraid to die. I just don't want to be there when it happens.'
Woody Allen